Presented to the

Ironside Memorial Library

by

Daniel Rosenberger

TIGER IN THE STREETS

TIGER IN THE STREETS

By WILLIAM ALAN BALES

ILLUSTRATED

DODD, MEAD & COMPANY   NEW YORK

1962

231

For Sydney

INTRODUCTION

This is the history of a city during a period of distress. It is a true story, gleaned from the newspapers of the period and the comments of those who witnessed the incidents described. I acknowledge an enormous debt to Horace Greeley, the taciturn and eminently responsible editor of the *New York Tribune* from 1841 to 1872, and to his professional rival, James Gordon Bennett of the *New York Herald*. They were the leaders, or at least the most prominent exemplars, of a style of journalism which, in its purest form, could not survive their century. They had their faults, both private and professional, but to their glory they both, in dramatically different ways, in pain and anger, sometimes wise and sometimes foolish, worked out the splendid rules that still govern American journalism. It is customary in an introduction for an author to acknowledge those "without whose help this book could not have been written." I acknowledge this debt freely and gladly, and, if I may, something more. I guess the word is "affection." Sometimes after long hours poring over the yellowed and crumbling but exciting back copies of the *Tribune* or *Herald,* speedily contrived for one day alone and not for me, I would emerge from the library with the exhilarating feeling that I had been in the presence of a kind of greatness.

This, as I said, is the history of a city during a period of distress. It is in some ways unfulfilling. History always is. And I suppose a good fiction writer could tidy it up. But truth, if it is occasionally disturbing, has a compulsion of its own. And what follows is not an account of what might have been or should have been. It is (and I shrink from my audacity) the way it was.

WILLIAM ALAN BALES

Locust Valley, N. Y.

CONTENTS

ILLUSTRATIONS

PROLOGUE

THE RAIN BEGAN AT NINE in the morning. Most New Yorkers welcomed it. It had been a dry spring, warm for May, and the big drops splattered down on the pavements and cobblestone streets like some harsh benediction. It was the season's first thunderstorm. It came from the north, down the funnel of the Hudson Valley, announcing itself in the city with a low rumbling and quick flashes of light. Two buildings on Eighth Avenue were struck by lightning. A band concert scheduled for Madison Square Park that evening might have to be postponed. And, down in the old Five Points area, gutters backed up and made miniature lakes at the curbs. No matter. It was a good rain and welcome.

Rain splashed against the windows of the big house on the southeast corner of Fifth Avenue and Forty-third Street. Mary Amelia Tweed, twenty-one years old and dark-haired, watched nervously, hoping it would clear before evening. This was her wedding day—May 31, 1871. Already the big floral wreath with the letters M and T had been set up in the big living room. The M stood for McGinnis—Arthur Mc-Ginnis, the groom. He was twenty-five and a widower.

Everything was in perfect order. The wedding gown was completed and delivered, and the Press had been informed of its cost—$5,000. The bride's father had engaged Mr. Eustice

1

Roberts to design and cut the trousseau and he had been told not to worry about the cost. He hadn't. It came to over $7,000. But the old man was pleased. "Make it the richest yet," he had said, "and fit for a princess." Some things you have to do big.

William Marcy Tweed. He was used to doing things big. He thought big and looked big. Five feet, eleven inches tall, a huge egg-shaped head and a waistline that shows the effects of too many roast duck and beef and oyster dinners with Jim Fisk and Jay Gould and people who want jobs with the city and will pay for them. There are scrubby side-whiskers climaxed in a full white-flecked growth at the chin. He has a mustache, a prominent, rounded nose, deep, penetrating eyes and full brows. He looks a little like a shrewd and calculating Santa Claus. He is Commissioner of Public Works for the City of New York, a director of the Erie Railroad and a state senator. He is also Grand Sachem of Tammany. He determines who shall be mayor of New York City and who shall be governor. Bills pass in the state legislature, or die, as he determines. And he has plans for picking the next President of the United States. He has worked hard in his forty-eight years. He has made many friends and stolen a lot of money—probably more than anyone else in the history of the country. When it's all over estimates of the extent of his thefts will vary.

Those who liked him and remembered him with affection said it probably wasn't more than twenty million dollars. But you didn't talk about that then. It wouldn't have done any good, and it was dangerous. Tweed also owned two out of the three judges on the state Supreme Court bench.

He didn't know it, of course, but he was the progenitor of what would soon emerge as a new species in American public life. It was almost as though some dark mutation, until now without significance, would, through him, acquire importance for the survival of his kind. There had been shrewd men before and men with daring and contempt for prevailing morality. But with Tweed these qualities would cease to be a purely personal phenomenon and acquire significance that was social and corporate.

In 1871, the art of local government was in a metamorphic stage in many places in America. The philosophy and many of the patterns evolved when the country was almost entirely agrarian still obtained, if not realistically, at least sentimentally. A short half-century before, local government in most eastern cities had still been the self-assumed responsibility of what might be called talented amateurs: men, usually of dignity and responsibility, whose personal affairs were in such order that they had time to concern themselves with the political machinery in their community. Frequently, of course, there were personal advantages to this, but they themselves looked upon their role as one of self-assumed responsibility. It was understandable in terms of noblesse oblige. It was a sort of benevolent despotism, time-consuming and frequently onerous, but, as in the education and discipline of children, eminently proper and essential.

But all that was changed now. At least in the big cities of the East. Tweed had helped to bring about the change. And it was a needed one. History was on his side. Viewed casually that spring of 1871, he would have seemed monolithic and unassailable. But he wasn't. He was a thief and furtive. And already he was being watched. *The New York Times* had been saying some devastating things in its editorials. But Tweed didn't care. *The Times* had no proof of any wrongdoing and he knew it. Just another newspaper editor sounding off. If it got annoying enough maybe he would have to pay them something . . .

The rain eased up by midmorning. But it stayed cool—62 degrees in contrast to yesterday's sweltering $92\frac{1}{2}$ degrees.

A fog rolled in off the river and was not dispelled by a fresh northerly breeze. But anything was better than yesterday's heat. Decoration Day, it had been, and the papers of May 31 gave the story a big play. There were impressive ceremonies down at Union Square. There was a parade with a band and that evening, speeches and recitations. The *Tribune* man turned in a nice piece of copy that night. Mr. Greeley adjusted his glasses and quickly marked the copy. Horace Greeley . . . getting along now. He might have led the fight against Tweed instead of those fellows over at *The Times*. Everything they knew about the newspaper business they learned from him. He had been in a score of fights in his career. But he would miss this one. There were those who said that he had presidential ambitions. If so, it's the better part of wisdom not to offend a big group like Tammany. But to business: ". . . the soldier dead of New York were honored yesterday by a very large representation from a warm-hearted, prosperous and grateful people."

Warm-hearted, prosperous and grateful people? Well, Mr. Greeley was getting along. He was sixty now and he had been in this business since he was fourteen. Maybe he just didn't see things as clearly as he once did. And maybe that was James Gordon Bennett's problem, too. He was seventy-six. The *Herald* had grown hugely since he worried out the first edition back in 1835. And, in his own way, he had remained true to the almost defiant promise he had made to his readers in that first edition: "We shall support no party, be the agent of no faction or coterie, and care nothing for any election, or any candidate from president down to constable."

They might have led the fight against Tweed, these two. But there had been so many fights and time was short. Both would die the next year.

Swiftly Greeley marked the copy for tomorrow's paper: "Music was by the Governor's Island Band. William H. Pope

recited 'The Raising of the Flag.'" Greeley was pleased. This
was the kind of story he liked. People behaving themselves.
Mr. Pope delighted the audience and was called back to the
rostrum. For an encore, he recited a poem called "You Have
Put No Flowers on My Papa's Grave."

At three the rain came down in earnest. For a full hour it
virtually pelted the city. Theater owners sighed and resigned
themselves to a slow evening. Too bad. There were some
interesting performances scheduled. *A Winter's Tale* was at
the Booth Theater at Twenty-third Street and Sixth Avenue.
Kit, or the Arkansas Traveller was at Niblo's Garden. And
at the Olympic Theater, *Jack Sheppard*. This was the story
of a convict who escaped from prison. It was an adventure
story based on a real escape. But of course such things didn't
happen these days. Not to anyone important. Prison? It was
a story from long ago and far away.

Like Cherry Street. Tweed was born there. Number One
Cherry Street. Not much of a house. Not bad, but—well,
what would his father have thought if he had seen this new
house on Fifth Avenue? Especially tonight. Flowers, all from
the Tweed place in Connecticut, were rampant throughout
the downstairs rooms. The bride and groom would receive
their guests standing before a floral decoration contrived in
the form of an American shield. Tweed liked that. He liked
the symbolism. And there were flowers everywhere. A huge
star of flowers hung over the doorway of the reception room;
flowers even in the knight's armor that held up chandeliers
on the stairway landings.

And the gifts! There were $700,000 worth. There were
forty pieces of jewelry of which fifteen were diamond sets.
One set alone cost $45,000. State Senator and Mrs. Henry
W. Genet were most gracious. They sent a cross made of
diamonds the size of peas. James H. Ingersoll, who had a
very thriving business going with the city, expressed a special

fondness for the bride and groom, sending a pin of sixty diamonds which, for some reason, were arranged in the shape of a sickle and sheaves of wheat. Jim Fisk's offering was especially dramatic. It was a frosted silver contrivance representing an iceberg and roughly the same size. It was apparently intended to hold ice cream. Molded silver bears rested on the handles and climbed up the silver spoons. It was bizarre but not unique. Police Commissioner James Kelso sent an exact duplicate.

Cherry Street. It was long ago and far away. Tweed could still summon up, though, the smell of glue in his father's upholstery shop. And the sounds . . . a creaking cart in the roadway. Children's voices on a spring night.

Cherry Street on a spring night. He could walk there in an hour but it seemed half a world away. And that paragraph that caught his eye in this morning's *Times*. Somehow it kept intruding even in the confusion of the wedding preparations. It wasn't important, really: "At about eight o'clock last evening as Anself Eschbacker was carrying his child, Anna, eighteen months old, through the hallway of his residence at 110 Cherry Street, Philip Pasquay, a fellow tenant who had been lying wait in the dark, suddenly attacked him and inflicted three severe but not dangerous wounds in the back and head with a murderous-looking knife. The babe was also severely stabbed over the eye. The trouble originated in the . . ."

110 Cherry Street. He knew the very house. It was across the street and up a bit from where he had lived. People were always fighting there. They had even in his day, and it had been a perfectly respectable neighborhood then. Well, he couldn't take on everybody's troubles even if they did happen to live in the old neighborhood.

Suddenly the flutterings of the ladies of the house told him it was time to start for the church. Trinity Chapel on West

Twenty-fifth Street. There was a crowd at the church door, of course. And they had come, not to see the bride but the "Boss."

There was a moment of confused whispering in the church lobby and then there they were, Mary Amelia and her father, walking slowly down the long aisle that stretched out below a giant, colored window high in the church wall. There was an audible hum even over the music at the bride's dress. It was white, corded silk, decolleté, with demi-sleeves and an immense court train. She wore a brooch of diamonds on her bosom. In each ear were three long pendants, set with three large solitaire diamonds. Her shoes, which barely showed, had diamond buttons. Slowly they walked and solemnly, past the congregation, past the Byzantine-like murals painted on both walls: Judas slinking from the Last Supper; "Thou Shalt Love Thy God. None Other Shalt Thou Serve." Waiting for them at the altar was the Reverend Joseph H. Price, stooped now and gray. He and Tweed, eyes meeting, remembered another spring twenty-seven years before when Tweed was the groom and the same Mr. Price had said the same words and the same prayers: "Who gives this woman . . . ?"

Tweed stepped back and into the pew at his left. He had never been quite comfortable in the Episcopal Church. So much form and ceremony. You always felt someone was watching you with disapproval. On the wall to his left, almost over his shoulder, was a mural of Christ in the Wilderness. And the words: "Man doth not live by bread alone." Tweed probably never noticed it.

Then they were playing music again and Mary Amelia and her husband were walking back up the aisle. Tweed next with Mrs. Tweed. Now for the reception. It would be a good one. Delmonico's had handled the supper arrangements . . . That business down at Cherry Street in this morning's paper. He'd send one of the boys from the Fourth Ward over there to look into it. Maybe they could help. Maybe some money would help. You could do almost anything with money. At least you could in this town.

It took a special detachment of police to control the crowd that jammed the sidewalks in front of the Tweed home. And it was something to see! Lights from top to bottom. A Brussels carpet had been rolled out over the sidewalk and a canopy set up. There were fountains at the side of the house. It rivaled even the big Restell place up on Fifty-second Street. Madame Restell had one of the finest houses on Fifth Avenue. She was an abortionist. Neighborhood children learned to spot her carriage with its liveried footmen. "Madame Killer!" they would shout. It was that kind of city and that kind of time.

Cheers for the Boss as he gets out of the carriage and walks, smiling, to the door. He turns and waves to the crowd and the cheers increase. And no one says: "Look, he uses the police as his special servants. He buys judges. He hires hoodlums to keep people away from the ballot box on Election Day. He has stolen millions and he wants more. He is a symbol of how democracy can fail. Look at him and see the weakness in ourselves."

No one said that. They said: "Look, the Boss takes care of everything. Even the rain has stopped."

It had. It was a lovely evening, and down in Madison Square Park, the band concert went on as scheduled.

And in Brooklyn that night, a fifteen-year-old boy named William Patterson prepared himself for a three-month term in the penitentiary. He had stolen fifty cents.

CHAPTER 1

OF BIRTH AND DEATH

"If we are not reformed by these things, we shall be yet more
awfully punished. Dreadful as has been the past calamity,
more dreadful calamities will be at hand."
— From a sermon preached in the Middle
Dutch Church, New York, November
17, 1822.

DURING THE EARLY EVENING of July 10, 1822, an eleven-
year-old girl named Amanda Reder, who lived with her family in a neat, airy, two-story brick house on New York's
Rector Street, complained to her mother that she was not
feeling well.

Her mother probably blamed the heat. It had been dreadful for weeks. There had been rain but it hadn't seemed to
help much, and many of New York's one hundred and thirty
thousand inhabitants had already sought the country. The
Reders had decided—or at least were forced—to stay. Martin
Reder was a barrel maker and apparently a good business-
man. His house was on one of the best streets on the west
side of the city. There were trees along the curb, and breezes
from the North River blew constantly. It was a good place
to raise children. There were three in the Reder family:
Amanda; John, seventeen; and Caroline who was nine.

Amanda couldn't describe what was wrong with her. She just felt sickish. Her mother put her to bed. A tonic might be called for if she still felt bad by morning. Meanwhile, the other children were to keep as quiet as possible so Amanda could sleep. There didn't seem to be any need for a doctor. It was the heat, and probably indigestion.

Later in the evening when Caroline began to complain of nausea, Mrs. Reder wasn't sure whether she was really ill or just jealous of the attention Amanda was getting. But Caroline, too, was put to bed. The lights were blown out upstairs and the house was quiet. To the east the Reders could hear the rumble of Broadway which, even in 1822, was never entirely at rest. There was an occasional boat horn from the river, and the distant voices of all hot summer nights. And the hum of those pesky mosquitoes. They bred in the swamps over on the East Side. And they seemed worse this year. So much rain. Well, maybe the girls would feel better in the morning.

They did not. They were irritable, nauseated and could eat nothing. All they wanted was water. Their mother kept them in bed and told them to sleep. They did, but fitfully and with troubled dreams. At supper time they were no better. The Reders called a doctor.

He was Daniel D. Walters, physician and druggist, who lived within walking distance of Rector Street. He examined the children and found them suffering from a fever. But the extremities were cool. There was some redness of the eyeballs and both children complained of dryness of the mouth. Dr. Walters made no diagnosis but said he would return.

He did. The next day. The symptoms were the same. Only the fever was more intense. He suggested a vinegar rub for both. What was the trouble? Well, it was too early to say.

The next day was a Saturday. It rained and Dr. Walters

did not visit the house on Rector Street. He stayed home with his long, dark thoughts.

But he was back at ten o'clock Sunday morning. Mrs. Reder was encouraged. The fever had broken in both children. They were quite cool to the touch. Dr. Walters reserved comment. He was concerned with a symptom Mrs. Reder had not noticed. The eyes, neck and breast of each child had become faintly tinged with yellow. And there was a hint of bleeding at the gums. Had either child vomited? Yes—Caroline. Rather severely. It seemed to be a black bile-like substance.

It was probably then that Dr. Walters made his reluctant diagnosis: yellow fever. It couldn't be anything else. It had visited the city three years before, breaking out in the low, swampy land to the east. And there had been two bad epidemics at the turn of the century. And now here it was again in this pleasant brick house on Rector Street.

Yellow fever. There was no cure, of course. And no one knew by what avenues it entered the city. But it passed somehow from person to person and made of each passerby an enemy. Just for him to speak the phrase meant that fear would stalk down every street and be the constant companion of every person.

It was a doctor's duty, of course, to advise the Board of Health of his diagnosis. But Dr. Walters hesitated. It was too momentous a decision to make quickly. Maybe the children would recover after all. Maybe he was wrong.

On Monday, Amanda seemed perhaps a little better. But little Caroline was worse. Caroline was dying.

Tuesday, July 16th, Dr. Walters was back at the Reder house. And there was more bad news. John this time. It seemed to be the same dreadful thing the girls had. Same symptoms. And time was running out.

Dr. Walters went straight to City Hall where either his

urgent manner or professional standing got him an immediate audience with the Mayor. And still he hedged.

"Sir, there are three cases of fever under my charge which I think demand the attention of the Board of Health."

He had still not said the dreaded phrase. And the Mayor was courteous but undisturbed. Mayor Stephen Allen. He was a sailmaker and a Whig. He had been appointed mayor by the Governor. And one imagines there were moments when he regretted his polite, formal words to the effect that he was both pleased and honored at the appointment. Sooner or later everyone with a problem seemed to come to his office. Traffic on Broadway, bad drainage on the filled-in land over the old Collect Pond. And now this excited doctor . . .

"What kind or description of fever do you think they have, Doctor?"

Now was the time. Dr. Walters couldn't quite make it.

"I think it such a fever as our soil and climate are not calculated to produce . . . a fever depending upon the introduction of foreign poison for its origin, and exotic in our country."

The Mayor decided that the resident physician of the Board of Health should accompany Dr. Walters to the Rector Street house. Perhaps together they could arrive at a more precise diagnosis. Meanwhile, Doctor, thank you for your comments . . .

Dr. N. J. Quackenbos, resident physician to the Board of Health, was duly advised. Without waiting for Dr. Walters to accompany him, he visited the Reders. Later that afternoon he met with the Mayor. The children, he said, were suffering from "bilious fever." No need for undue alarm.

The Mayor was relieved. There was enough trouble in the city without inventing things. Have you seen today's newspaper, Doctor? Fifteen city prisoners, sent out to work on the roads, escaped their dunderhead guards and took with them tools and chains to the value of eighty dollars! We haven't heard the last of this, you can be sure . . .

A wandering pig attacked a boy on Broome Street and injured him severely. And there was much shaking of heads over the news from Harrisburg. A number of outraged citizens had banded together and destroyed "six or seven houses of ill fame." The editor admitted that it was a matter of surprise and regret that "in so small a place there were so many places of that description to destroy."

There were letters to the editor in that evening's mail speculating on the number of such places that there might be in New York and one reader suggested that a count be taken. The editor was delighted with the suggestion. He knew a good story when he saw one . . .

Caroline died that night. And, in a ward in New York Hospital, a young man named Andrew Thomas also died. His illness was not specified and became significant only later. He was, he had told hospital authorities, a clerk in a grocery store. And the address? Rector Street.

John Reder died six days later, on the 22nd.

There were rumblings in the city by that time and shaking of heads. Parents ordered their children to avoid Rector Street, and cartmen grumbled when dispatched into the area. The news of John Reder's death came to the attention of the editor of the *New York Spectator* and he dispatched a reporter to City Hall to nose around and see what he could turn up. It was an unexciting story that he turned in for the next day's edition: "The Board of Health of this city met yesterday and resolved to meet hereafter every Monday at four o'clock P.M. This city, it was understood, has never been more healthy at this season of the year than at present."

It was slim consolation to the Reders and their now thoroughly frightened neighbors. And no one was relieved by a laconic announcement that came within a few days from the Board of Health. One Leonard Archer, neighbor to the Reders, was under observation. The diagnosis: bilious fever.

Then there was old John Hamilton who sold fruit and vegetables from his cart on Rector Street. He had been missing for several days from his accustomed post. Someone made inquiries. The Board of Health knew all about it. A case of bilious fever . . .

There were other cases. A Dr. Neilson went before the board and for the first time spoke the dreaded words: two cases of yellow fever at the corner of Rector and Greenwich Streets. But there was a private consultation and he agreed to change his diagnosis. It was malignant bilious fever. All nodded agreement. No need for alarm. Wild stories and rumors could start a panic. People would leave the city in droves. Thousands of dollars would be lost because of irresponsible talk.

And the news, diminished and qualified, came first, not from the Board of Health, but from a newspaper editor. It was August first, three weeks after Amanda's illness: "From all we have been able to learn, we are of the opinion that the city had been visited with several cases of yellow fever. However, we do not think there is cause of alarm out of the infected area."

But before the paper went to press, a late-breaking development had to be quickly inserted. Small type was used because there was not enough space: "Leonard Archer, mentioned in the Board of Health report of yesterday, died this morning with every symptom of a strong and decided case of yellow fever."

A delegation waited upon Dr. Quackenbos. What, Sir, is the real situation? Three days later the statement came. And it was made reluctantly and with ill grace: ". . . it is evident that the cause or causes that at first were only sufficient to produce bilious fever have now become so concentrated as to produce yellow fever." This was duly reported in the *Spectator* that night. And the editor added a plaintive note of his own: "We trust God in His mercy will arrest the arm of the destroying angel and save us from the pestilence which destroyeth in darkness and wasteth at noon day."

And the fear settled down over the city. And each person reacted after his own fashion. Some went to church to offer prayers for deliverance. Some made grotesque jokes about the fever and, on meeting a friend on the street, would pretend to have "the shakes." There was revelry in the Bowery taverns. But the laughter was strained, and no amount of rum or whisky could entirely dispel the feeling that someone was staring over your shoulder.

As many as could left the city for the healthier atmosphere further uptown. By dawn of the 10th, Broadway and all the streets leading north were jammed with carts, wagons—anything that could move. The travelers jostled each other in their speed but there were few arguments. There just wasn't time. All day the sombre procession rolled up the streets. And at nightfall there was no lessening. It was as though all were fleeing an enemy all the more fearsome for being invisible.

The Board of Health began issuing orders as though to make up for its laxness. It was announced that all residents in a three-block area around Rector Street would have to leave their homes so that the streets could be boarded up. It was promptly done. There was comfort somehow in the sound of the hammers, as though the evil thing that was born there could be held back by walls. No one was allowed to enter except the watch. And suddenly a whole neighborhood surrendered to the enemy. It stood silent and deserted by day, but at night it was alive with the sound of a curious conflict.

Cats. Most of the families there had kept them because of

the rats that sometimes came up from the banks of the river. And in their haste to leave, many of the owners forgot their cats. Scores of them swarmed through the empty streets, leaping up toward the walls in an attempt to escape and filling the night with their sounds. For awhile, what must have been a swift and terrible warfare took place and the rats were killed. Some of the cats probably managed to break open forgotten boxes of food. But most of them went hungry. The watch, checking the ramparts of the fearsome neighborhood, would spot them occasionally. They traveled, uncat-like, in packs. One watchman reported that they "screamed" for food and another, venturing into the tiny and tremendous streets, told how one giant cat detached itself from a pack and leapt at him with jaws wide open.

And there was another marauder. An unemployed sailor was arrested in the boarded-up area. He had scrambled over a fence, taking his chances on the disease in the hope of finding valuables left behind. But he stole nothing. The watch, hearing firing in the area late at night, entered and caught —or rather rescued—the intruder. He was standing in the middle of the street, firing in horror at the cats. But for the most part the whole area was deserted except for the cats, the slow-crossing of the sun, and the winds that blew refuse along the street and billowed the curtains out of open windows like some desperate signal of distress.

By September 5th it was apparent that the disease was moving north and east. There was a case of the fever on Liberty Street. Then one on New Street, just south of Wall. Then Pearl Street. And on September 23rd, a man named Henry Brush, a pumpmaker, died of the fever in his home on the corner of Cherry and Pelham Streets.

This was not far from the home of a chairmaker named Richard Tweed who lived with his family in a house at Number One Cherry Street. The street is almost lost now

under the abutments to the Brooklyn Bridge, but in 1822 it
was a respectable neighborhood of private homes and the
modest shops of craftsmen. And the house at Number One
Cherry Street had a special significance. It was built on the
site of the very grand building where President Washington
had lived when New York was the federal capital. The
neighborhood had diminished considerably since then, and
already New York society had started its long trek uptown.
But Cherry Street still showed some evidence of its one-time
grandeur. The president of the newly formed New York Gas
Company, for example, lived at Number Seven Cherry
Street. And there was a rumor that the next year his whole
house was going to be lit by gas.

For three generations now, the Tweeds had lived in the
almost village-like east side of New York. In the middle of
the eighteenth century, the first Tweed and his bride had
migrated from the little village of Kelso on the banks of the
Tweed River in Scotland. They settled on Rutgers Street to
the east of the commons where the first Tweed set up a
blacksmith shop. There were two sons, Robert and Philip,
both of whom were also blacksmiths. Philip frequently shod
the horses of one Thomas Ash, a chairmaker whose shop was
in a charming old building adjoining the Methodist Meeting
House on John Street. Ash was an important man. He was
foreman in the Fire Department and a treasurer of the newly
formed Tammany Society. No mere blacksmith, of course,
could aspire to such honors. But Philip's son might. And so
Richard Tweed was taught a genteel craft. And eventually
it was Richard Tweed, maker of chairs, and—his father
hoped—politician-to-be.

His hopes were never realized. Richard Tweed was not
Thomas Ash. He would never be a fire department foreman
nor an official of Tammany Hall. Still, he was modestly successful in his chairmaking business. He had a nice house and

a good family, and his early ambitions could be centered now on his children. There were four in the little house at One Cherry Street—two boys and two girls. And even as the news came that yellow fever was abroad in the city, his wife, Eliza, informed him that a fifth child was on the way. Next April.

Richard wanted to move uptown. Many of his neighbors had already locked things up and moved away. But this involved considerable expense and many chairs would have to be made and sold to pay for such a move. A new shop would have to be rented. And living quarters for the family. So Richard and his family seem to have stayed. At least the list of businessmen who moved out does not include the name of Richard Tweed.

Most of the downtown churches closed. No services and, above all, no burials. There was strong feeling that the disease came from graves. Trinity Church on Broadway was the special subject of angry mutterings. It was the above-ground vaults. They said the air in the neighborhood of the churchyard was dank with the effusions. How can you expect the city to be healthy? No more burials. And throw lime on the graves already there . . .

The theaters closed or found make-shift premises uptown. The owners of the Park Theater surrendered, closed their doors and reluctantly announced that no performances would be given until the end of the epidemic. All public meetings, of course, were canceled.

The Tammany Hotel, owned by the Tammany Society, at Nassau and Frankfort Streets held out. There was an advertisement in the papers calling attention to its "salutary location, being on high and open ground and airy." This was not entirely true but no one ventured to challenge the statement. No one really cared. Tammany was not yet the powerful organization it would become. The man who would give it ultimate expression and power and meaning had not yet been born. In 1822, Tammany, although it had shown some influence in a number of local elections, was still a rather ill-defined, purposeless organization, given to parades and patriotic speeches and a rather naive dependency on ritual and self-conscious idiom. It had been founded in 1789 by a New York upholsterer named William Mooney. Mooney was a veteran of the Revolutionary War and intensely patriotic, although there had been rumors that at one time during the war he had become confused in his loyalties and served with the British. But all that was over now and no one had more hopes for the new country or contempt for the Tories than Mooney. In fact, the little group he organized and presided over in the first "wigwam" in a tavern on Broad Street was in a sense a protest group. On the dissolution of the American Army after the Revolution, there had been formed a group called the Society of the Cincinnati. The members were former officers in Washington's army. They tended to be aristocratic, Federalist in politics and followers of Hamilton rather than Jefferson. Further, the eldest son of each member enjoyed the rights of membership on the death of his father.

To many who had served in the ranks this seemed like the beginning of an "officer cult." It was undemocratic and European. The very name, "Society of the Cincinnati," had an ominous sound and unless one had read and remembered Roman history, it was meaningless and hence mysterious. William Mooney cast about for a better name for what he hoped would be a better group.

There was a legend during the eighteenth century revolving around the figure of one Tammany, Indian chief extraordinary. Actually, such a man had existed. In the 1680's, he had been chief of a tribe of Delaware Indians called the Lenni-Lenape whose main village was near the present site of Princeton, New Jersey. Tammany was one of the chiefs to welcome William Penn to this country in 1682. Whatever other virtues he had, charity was certainly an important one. It is recorded that he surrendered some three hundred square miles of real estate to Penn in return for assorted goods that could easily have been loaded on a single wagon.

But Tammany, whether it was his bearing or demeanor or some inherent quality that escapes us now, was one of those men who, across the centuries, is simply born to be a legend. By 1771, he emerges in American life as a saint and the personification of the noble savage. He had communication with the great spirit and was "a stranger to everything that is bad." He engaged the devil in combat and seems to have come out at least with a draw. Somewhere along the line he found time to discover corn, beans and crabapples. He also discovered tobacco but, saint-like, used it only to destroy fleas and drive away mosquitoes.

What he was really like probably no one will ever know. From a distance of three hundred years he seems like some bucolic Alger hero, constantly striving and succeeding and growing in nobility. His death was a little over-dramatic. All his wonders accomplished and with nothing but anticlimax staring him in the face, he wrapped himself in a blanket and set himself on fire.

He was an improbable saint. But it was an improbable time and to William Mooney he seemed like the perfect symbol of virtue. He was strong, brave, true and, perhaps above all, a native American. His only competitor for honors was Christopher Columbus, and there were apparently some who wanted to ditch Tammany in favor of the Navigator. But Columbus, after all, was a foreigner and had been hand and glove with royalty. So there was a compromise—the first in a long series of compromises that the Society would make across the centuries. In the spring of 1789, it was officially proclaimed that there had come into being The Society of St. Tammany or Columbian Order.

But there was more of Tammany than of Columbus in the new organization. It was divided into thirteen tribes, each presided over by a "sachem." There was also a "grand sachem" who, at the time of the organization, was Mooney himself. In the early years, the President of the United States was made Great Grand Sachem, or, as the early Tammanyites preferred to call him, "Kitchi Okemaw." There was a master of ceremonies called a Sagamore, and a doorkeeper who, if his duties were unpretentious, could at least glory in the title of "Wiskinskie."

In 1790, "Kitchi Okemaw" George Washington himself took advantage of the Indian rituals of Tammany. The government had been having trouble signing a peace treaty with the Creek Indians who occupied large tracts of land in Georgia and Florida. President Washington arranged for a Colonel Marinus Willett, a member of the newly organized Tammany Society and a hero of the Revolutionary War, to visit the Creek Indians and invite the chief to visit New York. The idea seems to have been to so impress the Indians with the power of the white man that they would become discouraged in their resistance to the settlers. The Creek chief was the son of a Scotch trader and an Indian woman and reveled in the name of Colonel Alexander McGillivray. He and twenty-eight of his braves accepted the invitation and set off for New York. General Washington was delighted but, as it turned out, the initial meeting with the Tammany men was hardly one to instill fear into the hearts of the Indian braves.

In anticipation of their arrival, the New Yorkers had set up wigwams on the shore of the Hudson River and dressed themselves in their fiercest Indian regalia. The real Indians, thinking for a moment that they were meeting their real brothers, dashed into the encampment with great shouts and waving of tomahawks. The Tammany braves took off in a body and, while official Tammany accounts of the incident are austere and abbreviated, there is indication that they didn't stop running until they got to Broadway.

Later, more restrained meetings were organized. There were sightseeing trips and long talks, and it was explained to McGillivray that "the spirits of Tammany and Columbus are walking backward and forward in the wigwam." This seems to have been an impressive point. At least the Indians signed a peace treaty and the border warfare ceased.

And Tammany had won considerable prestige. It lasted unimpaired until a certain sad day in 1809, when it was discovered that William Mooney, the now venerable founder, had been less than meticulous in his handling of certain city accounts. Mooney had been appointed superintendent of the City Almshouse at an annual salary of $1,000, with an additional $500 available for family expenses. An audit of the books by some killjoy revealed that Mooney had spent $4,000 a year and had drawn an additional $1,000 for supplies. The consumption of rum in the Almshouse had more than doubled; the use of brandy had increased four times and of gin six times.

Faced with the necessity of explaining all this, Mooney's defense was ingenious but ineffectual. The additional money, he said, had gone for "trifles for Mrs. Mooney."

By late September the fever possessed the city like an invading army. Hundreds of businesses were closed down. There were empty buildings on Broadway and whole streets where no one walked. There were shutters across windows and doors double-barred as though the intruder might at any moment ascend the steps and sound the knocker. Philadelphia announced that no one from New York would be admitted into the city. New Haven quickly followed suit.

Undertakers did a brisk business. So did the makers of "fever cures" and "bilious pills." Epsom salts was supposed to help and camomile tea was advised in the case of vomiting. The *New York Spectator* suggested taking "salt petre pounded, spread it on an earthen dish and pour oil of vitriol over."

But by far the most popular medication was a concoction called the "Vinegar of the Four Thieves." The vendors told an interesting story. In the mid-sixteenth century Marseilles had been visited by a plague similar to the one now in New York. The inhabitants fled, taking a stand in caves on the hills outside the city. But the city each day was visited by four hardy scoundrels who robbed at leisure and even had the gall to pass within sight of the homeowners on their trips in and out of the city. But no one dared molest them or even approach them because of the danger of infection. Finally, however, the sight of their valuables being carted away became overwhelming and a pitfall was devised. The robbers duly fell into the trap and were captured. One of them, bargaining for his life, offered to reveal the potion that permitted them to escape the plague. Thus was born the remedy known as the "Vinegar of the Four Thieves." It was sold by the gallon in New York in 1822 and more than one vendor became rich on the profits. Unfortunately the formula has not survived the times, but one contemporary New Yorker had an idea of its origin. "Where they got so much of this thievish vinegar I could never find out," he wrote years later, "but I strongly suspect it was made from crab-apples by some of them Hackensack farmers in the Jerseys."

On September 28th it is duly recorded that a woman named Mrs. Sarah Claar died of the fever at Seventy-five Cherry Street. The news must have sent chills up the spine of Richard Tweed. Number Seventy-five was within a few minutes walk of his own little shop at Twenty-four Cherry.

On October 19th another death on Cherry Street. It was a man named Samuel Reed. Chances are that Tweed knew him. It's almost certain that he heard of his death.

We can imagine the scenes in the little house on Cherry Street. Daily examinations of the children, concern for the mother now expecting her fifth child, and the prayers for cold weather.

It came suddenly. It was mid-October and almost overnight the warm weather ended and a frost came to the city. On October 26th the *Spectator,* almost cautiously, announced: "Neither a new case nor a death to be reported from yellow fever this day."

The next day clouds began to gather over the city from the northeast. By mid-afternoon a chilly rain began to fall and the wind picked up. By dusk gales of wind were sweeping across the city, driving the rain in sheets as if to cleanse the city of infection.

There was a gradual clearing by the next morning, and on Broadway an unaccustomed sound, a wagon rolling down to the lower city from the north. There was a second and a third and by nightfall it was practically a procession. In the next few days boards were taken down from the windows, rooms were aired out carefully and the fencing was ripped away from the Rector Street crossroads.

The epidemic was over.

Amanda Reder, who was the first to contract the fever, survived.

There was speculation as to the cause of yellow fever for awhile and discussion as to the manner of treatment. But in a surprisingly short time the incident seems to have been almost forgotten. Theaters reopened. Shops inserted advertisements in the papers promising reductions because of inventory and the city returned to its destiny.

But the incidents of that summer were not entirely forgotten. On Sunday, November 17th, the Reverend Paschal N. Strong stood before his congregation in the Dutch Reformed Church. He took as his text Leviticus 26: 23—24: "If ye will not be reformed by me by these things, but will walk contrary unto me; then will I also walk contrary unto you, and will punish you yet seven times for your sins."

He pauses for a moment and regards his congregation. There is not one there who mistakes what the punishment was . . .

"God then was pleased to send upon our city the pestilence . . . a pestilence highly contagious, voracious in its thirst for prey, rapid in its work of death, dreadfully malignant . . . spreading from person to person, from house to house, from street to street, scattering dismay and horror as it approached, causing all to flee before it . . ."

Over a thousand persons had died between July 26th and November 2nd. The good had died, and the evil. Old people had died, and children. And no one knew why.

"Now, brethren, wherefore was all this? Why has this evil come upon us? How is it that such wrath has gone out against this city from the Lord? Surely he doth not willingly afflict nor grieve the children of men . . ."

The Reverend Mr. Strong had an answer: appetite for gain, love of pleasure, profligacy of morals and "a spirit of political feeling at war with the authority of God . . ."

The congregation was stilled. You could hear its corporate breathing. Mr. Strong was near the end. We can fancy beads of perspiration on his brow despite the coolness of the church. He would never reach these heights again.

"If we are not reformed by these things, we shall be yet more awfully punished. Dreadful as has been the past calamity, more dreadful calamities will be at hand."

And there were those in the congregation who would live

to see the prophecy come true. They would see New York in flames and more people killed in a single week than the fever had taken in a whole summer. They would see slums cultivated and nourished almost as though disease and crime and violence were things of civic pride. They would see wholesale thievery applauded as shrewdness, and ignorance and greed exalted in the name of democracy. They would see an oppressor hailed as a saviour and his detractors denounced as enemies of the state . . .

Eliza Tweed was in her third month now. It would be her fifth child. Surely the last. Richard was really not making enough money to support more children. Perhaps if he had not been forced to work so hard he would have had more time to realize the ambitions of his father. He might have gone into politics. Well, all is as God wills . . .

It was a very cold Christmas Eve and a slim one in the little house at One Cherry Street.

And that night, uptown and to the west, a young Greek professor trudged home from the poulterer's shop. Christmas Eve is a night for memories and he was thinking about a legend they used to tell around the fire when he was a boy in the rambling old house on Long Island. It was about St. Nicholas who was supposed to visit the homes of children and bring toys. It occurred to him that his own children had never heard that story.

Later that night, in his study, the professor began to write it all down. To intrigue his children even further he put it in verse:

His name was Clement Clarke Moore. He was a doctor of philosophy and a professor of Greek and Oriental studies at the Episcopal General Theological Seminary. He was a young man but his fame was secure. He had written a book called *A Compendious Lexicon of the Hebrew Language*. And this, surely, would not soon be forgotten. Meanwhile, this doggerel to amuse his children:

> " 'Twas the night before Christmas and all through the house,
> Not a creature was stirring, not even a mouse."

He didn't dream it then, but he would spend many years denying that he ever authored such a frivolous piece of writing. It was damaging to his professional career. What would happen to his *Compendious Lexicon?*

> "When out on the lawn there arose such a clatter,
> I sprang from my bed to see what was the matter . . ."

It was a long winter and spring came late. March was raw and cold as though winter were petulant about the turning of the seasons. There had been a few days with a hint of spring. But there was to be one final gesture.

It began Easter Sunday morning, the 30th of March. Early churchgoers noticed the long bank of sullen grey clouds that gathered to the north and east. And the wind picked up. By nine in the morning, snow was falling and by noon the wind had reached hurricane strength. All day it roared and ranted about the city and the snow beat down as if to mock the day. There were boats capsized in the Bay; others blown up on the beach at Staten Island. It was a wet, thick snow. And it fell all night. At two in the morning there was an alarm of fire in the lower city. Several companies turned out into the storm and dragged the engines to the scene.

It was a false alarm. It seemed appropriate, somehow. Things were out of joint. There should be no storm this late in the season. Everything was wrong. The old values were changing. It was not easy to tell friends from enemies these days. Even Tammany had changed. It was getting aristocratic, almost. Trouble was the young men who had started out with their dreams of a fuller democracy were now old. And furthermore, many of them had made money. They were beginning to think like rich men . . .

The giants who had led the country through the Revolution and the trying early days of the Republic were dead. And lesser men were taking their place. A canal linking the Great Lakes with the Hudson River would be opened in a couple of years. And New York would get bigger and louder and more crowded than ever.

Patches of snow were still on the ground that following Thursday. It was April 3, 1823. And on that day, in the small house at One Cherry Street, Eliza Tweed gave birth to her fifth and last child.

It was a boy and he was named William Marcy.

William Marcy Tweed. It was a curious selection, that name. And prophetic. It was natural that Richard with his thwarted ambitions would name his son after a politician. William Marcy was a prominent Democrat who, in 1823, held the post of comptroller of the State of New York. But he would achieve a fragile immortality years later because of a phrase in a speech he delivered in the United States Senate.

"To the victors," he said, "belong the spoils."

CHAPTER 2

SEEDS OF TIME

"If you can look into the seeds of time,
And say which grain will grow and which will not . . ."
— *Macbeth* I. iii, as performed at the
Astor Opera House, New York, May 10,
1849.

THEY WAITED THAT SPRING for the fever to come back. But it did not. June came and July and an August heavy with rain. But there was no fever. There were crowded sidewalks on Broadway and the Bowery, and carts rolling down Rector Street past the old Reder place. And after awhile everyone forgot. Almost everyone. Martin Reder did not forget. The house must have seemed hollow and haunted by remembered voices. The city directory has an impersonal comment on his sorrow. The Reders gave up the house some time in 1824 and moved to another down the block. The newspapers continued to print advice on how to avoid contagion, but such items took less and less space as the summer advanced and everyone seemed to feel certain that the time of plague was over and that evil of all kind had been forever banished from the city.

William Marcy Tweed was big even as a boy. It was good to be big on Cherry Street in those years. Already the street had lost its early grandeur. Too near the waterfront, the old residents were saying. Bursts of laughter in the late hours after decent people had gone to bed. Sailors, newly paid and restive, swaggered the street and asked passersby the way to the Bowery. And the women. Prim enough as they walked along, it seemed. But different too. They didn't avoid your gaze. And their errands seemed never to end. The nights pushed toward midnight and still they walked. Brazen creatures! Didn't they know that General Washington himself once lived on this street?

"Little Bill" he was called at first. He didn't like that, and after awhile it meant fight. And he was good at that. Stocky but quick and when he hit, he hit hard. After awhile they stopped calling him Little Bill. Suddenly it was "Big" Bill, and he probably never knew they were saying it in jest. He didn't get jokes as well as some . . . especially if the joke were on him.

And, of course, there was a boys' gang—the Cherry Hillers. And by the time he was twelve or so, Big Bill was the leader. They stole fruit from street carts and pigs' tails from the butcher stalls and fought with the Henry Street boys to the north. There were challenges formally presented and accepted. Big Bill always liked such occasions, especially when they involved him. He enjoyed winning. And by the age of twelve he had a philosophy. There was always a winner and a loser. Didn't you know that? There were no other questions that needed to be asked. "But the other boy had two stones in his fists! He didn't fight fair!" Big Bill could never quite get the point. He didn't understand excuses for losing. And he never would . . . There were winners and there were losers. It was as simple as that.

Big Bill learned to swagger, picked up some juvenile profanity, and went to school on Chrystie Street not far from his home. He was not a good student, but he was not entirely dull. They would say, striving to remember him in later years, that he was good at figures. But their memories may have been distorted by all that had happened since . . .

Bursts of laughter in the early hours on Cherry Street, and the whole city was changing. It was getting too big. Immigrant ships arrived almost daily. Strange languages. The old, aristocratic ways had gone out of fashion. On October 26, 1825, the Erie Canal was officially opened and the first boat began the trip from Buffalo to Albany and then down the Hudson to New York City and the Atlantic. From now on the produce of the West would find its way, too, to New York. And suddenly things that had happened only a decade ago, or even a year ago, were old-fashioned and quaint. There was a single day when the last remnant of the past ended almost as though a door had been closed and there was nothing more to say. It was May 23, 1836. Bill Tweed was thirteen years old.

On that day, in a big, rambling, old house near Rhinebeck, New York, a man named Edward Livingston died. At the turn of the century he had been mayor of New York and federal district attorney. He was an aristocrat—austere, remote, aloof, and he had gone through life as though keeping a rendezvous with history. In 1803, while he was mayor, a clerk he had appointed to keep accounts absconded with some federal funds. Livingston acted promptly and in the only way possible for one with his concept of personal and public conduct. He promptly resigned all offices and personally assumed the debt. It was $43,666.21. Twenty-three years later, he made the last payment. With interest it came to $100,014.19. He seemed to have thought his conduct in no way remarkable.

Livingston was equally demanding on others. A partisan wrote to him on one occasion, suggesting that an examination of State Department files would show that Henry Clay, their common enemy in politics, had once accepted valuable gifts from George III. Confirmation of this would have meant the end of Clay in politics. Would Mr. Livingston look into the matter? He would not. "I am politically opposed to Mr. Clay," he wrote, "but I am persuaded that he would never have done anything that would justify the imputation; and if such a report is current I should be sorry that even my silence should keep it alive. I am persuaded, Sir, that you agree with me in thinking that any political advantage, however great, would be bought too dear if obtained by countenancing such calumnies on our opponents."

There was a prescribed technique to stealing a pig's tail. It called for planning, organization and, on the part of one boy, a certain amount of nerve. One of the Cherry Hillers would be appointed to stand across the street from the butcher's stand and, while feigning an idle occupation such as whittling, to observe closely the position and general state of alertness of the butcher. Another boy, a sharp knife hidden behind his back, would saunter alongside the stand and wait for the signal to be given. Then he would dash forward, grab the pig carcass with one hand and, as quickly as possible, detach the tail. As in any assault, surprise and speed were the important factors. Tweed soon became an acknowledged master. He could slice off the tail with a single, well-rehearsed motion. A picnic and barbecue would always follow on the high ground around what is now Union Square where the statue of Washington observes with seeming distaste the random meetings of the city's discontent.

Potatoes, fruit, pigs' tails . . . it was boys' stuff and it was fun. There was a delicious element of danger in it, and the grown-up world made it quite clear that it was wrong. Most of the gang would grow up and find one day that they agreed. But there was no stopping them then. There was no stopping young Tweed, especially. He was the leader and he called the tune. A fight or a picnic or a swim off the docks of the East River? It was Tweed who decided every time. The other boys gave up trying to assert independence or even to argue with him. He fought too well and he didn't enjoy having his leadership questioned. What began as suggestions soon turned into orders. A few of the boys dropped out. But most stayed and became satellites of the young leader. The truth was that life with Bill Tweed was exciting. And he was pleasant to be with as long as you didn't cross him. He was a good winner, never crowing over his adversaries nor reminding them of their failure. He won things charmingly. But he won.

Except at school. There were others who got better marks. And in supervised play periods it was determined, quite to the surprise of the other Cherry Hillers, that he really wasn't the fastest runner or the highest jumper. And at gymnastics he was in fact quite awkward.

When he was eleven, he quit school and became an apprentice in his father's shop.

William Tweed? He was a large boy, teachers would say later, trying to remember. Good at figures. A leader. Hard to control. Quick to fight. And there was no boy in school his age who dared stand up to him.

Not many years after Tweed left the little school on Chrystie Street, a new student arrived to take his place in the same classroom. One wonders if he ever sat at the same desk. His name was Thomas Nast. His family had recently immigrated from Landau, Germany. The two boys did not meet. Not then. Nast was not a leader, but he had an aptitude curiously well-developed in one so young. He could draw— fellow students, teachers, the head of a tiger—anything. He was a shy boy but friendly and appealing. He couldn't fight very well. Not with his fists. But he could draw pictures—

vicious pictures of the people he didn't like. And he didn't
like bullies.

Tweed ran errands for his father, did a few chores, but
most of his time was spent bossing the Cherry Hillers. Maybe,
when he was older, he could join a real gang. When you belonged to a real gang, you were important.

He was right. In 1834, New Yorkers elected their mayor
for the first time. Previous mayors had been appointed by
a committee in Albany. And, as there were no registration
laws, it was easy to vote. It was easy to vote several times.
Both parties encouraged this. The Whigs did it. But Tammany, being better organized, did it better. And slowly and
subtly the control of the city passed from the old and usually
wealthy Dutch-English amateur politicians to the ward boss
and the gang leader. After 1834 the affairs of the city were
determined, not in the gentlemen's club, but the saloon. For
better or for worse, the men who had built the city would
now govern it. Across the years they would love it, debase it,
steal from it. Some would have to flee from it. But they would
govern it. Or, at least, they'd try.

And the gang became important. There had long been
gangs in New York—informal groupings of idle young men
who originally had importance in the neighborhood whose
streets they stalked with proprietary arrogance. But now it
was different. Any gang leader worth his salt could tell his
boys how to vote. He was useful in any number of ways. He
or his boys could run errands. He could express official policy
in an unofficial way. And, perhaps best of all, he didn't have
to be invented. He was simply already there.

New York's first gangs were bred in the dark and swampy
slums of the Five Points, a squalid, tubercular, rat-infested
area where three streets met in a little open place as though
they had become confused in their wanderings and were
seeking air. Here were born the Roach Guards, the Chin-

chesters and the Plug Uglies who wore enormous hats stuffed
with cotton as helmets and who, before they faded from history, gave a new name to violence. There were the Shirt
Tails who sailed into battle with their shirts out—a refine-
ment that was looked on as rather effete by other gang members who usually fought in their undershirts. And from the
Five Points came perhaps the worst gang of all, the Dead
Rabbits. In the patois of the time, a "rabbit" was a rowdy.
And a "dead rabbit" was the most dangerous rowdy of all.

The Dead Rabbits had originally been a part of the Roach
Guards, so named after the obliging grocery and liquor
dealer whose shop served as their meeting place. Internal
dissension developed during one gang meeting and someone
threw a dead rabbit into the center of the room. It was taken
as an omen. The dissenters withdrew, their emblem already
chosen. In subsequent brawls they marched proudly behind
a long standard on which was impaled a dead rabbit.

Their brawls were frequent and violent and inconclusive.
Occasionally they would be joined by the ladies who took
charge of the gentler aspects of the fighting. Piling paving
blocks at strategic places, for example. Or giving the alarm
when the military were turned out. But there was one whose
spirited conduct during moments of emergencies was such
that she was adored by all who knew her. She was called
"Hell-Cat Maggie" and unfortunately no proper description
of her exists except the rather stern adjective, "angular." But
she must have had a certain charm. At least, for the Dead
Rabbits. It is recorded that she filed her teeth to sharp points
and devised long brass fingernails, all of which she used un-
stintingly in furtherance of the group's community projects.
Occasionally the state guard and even the regular army had
to be summoned to help curb Maggie and her friends when
they sallied out in search of an evening's diversion. And it's
not always recorded who won the contest.

There is a small, well-ordered, well-manicured park now in the center of Maggie's old neighborhood. Children from nearby Chinatown and the Italian district of Mulberry Street play there in complete amity. Perhaps it's just as well that Maggie has long since disappeared from the scene. She would be shocked and hurt to see how the old traditions are flaunted. She was, they say, intensely sentimental.

And the Bowery had a gang. "The Bowery B'hoys" they were called. They fought with the Five Pointers, plastered their hair with Batcheler's Celebrated Hair Dye and walked the street as if they owned it, which, in effect, they did.

The Bowery Boy of this period was fairly easy to recognize, largely because he wanted it that way. He almost invariably wore a fireman's red flannel shirt, fastened well to one side with large white buttons. The number of the fire company was usually appliqued or embroidered on the shirt. There was a silk tie, black and carelessly tied, black broadcloth pantaloons tight to the knees and then flaring out to the bottoms, tight calf-skin boots with high heels, and a black stove-pipe hat invariably worn pitched forward so that the brim almost touched the cigar tilted upward in the wearer's teeth. He walked with an exaggerated, rolling gait which he felt was suggestive of powerful musculature but was more probably thrust upon him by his high-heeled and frequently uncomfortable boots. His girl looked like a caricature of the fashionable ladies uptown. Her skirt was shorter and fuller, color combinations were selected for their dazzling effect, and her hat had a floppier brim and gaudier trimmings. She wore her hair combed back and caught in long cork-screw curls which fell to her shoulders. And her walk was an imitation of her B'hoy's. In winter she carried a muff of imitation fur.

The Bowery was their street. They were uncomfortable in any other neighborhood and resented the intrusion of society folk in their territory. They had a certain clan feeling and they took care of their own. The B'hoys were not criminals. Not yet. They worked as butchers, drovers, longshoremen, and they could put out fires better than anyone else. But they needed a leader. Someone to give them unity of purpose and importance. That duty fell to a broad-shouldered, violent, deeply scarred man named Isaiah Rynders of Tammany Hall.

Rynders came to New York in the early 1840's. He had been a gambler on Mississippi River boats, but by the time he got east the story was that he had been a river boat captain. At least he assumed that title and was so addressed. About 1843, Rynders organized the Empire Club, a loose confederation of saloon keepers and such, which became the political center of the Sixth Ward—the "Bloody Auld Sixth," as it was beginning to be called. To this place came eventually all who had business to transact along the Bowery or in the slums of the Five Points. A building going up or coming down? A store to be opened? You had to deal with Rynders. There simply was no other authority. The gang leaders paid tribute to him as the Sixth Ward leader in Tammany and he, in turn, kept them out of trouble. He got jobs for their sons if they were hard-working and conscientious, or he bailed them out if they were not. He asked no questions except at election time. And then he asked just one. Will you vote the Tammany ticket?

Most of the Sixth Ward did. It would have been unrealistic to have voted any other way. Residents of the Sixth Ward seldom saw a representative of the Whig Party. Tammany was all around them. Tammany helped them. It gave them food. Money, too, sometimes. If Rynders and the others shake down prostitutes occasionally or allow a pickpocket to work unmolested for a kick-back . . . well, they're doing it for us, aren't they? That time last winter when we ran out of fuel. Who showed up with a bag of coal and some food, too? One of your holier-than-thou, nose-in-the-air Whigs? Not by a damned sight . . .

And so they voted for Tammany. And they were happy to. If an election were an important one, they were just as happy to vote three or four times. In the depression that followed the great fire of 1835, a Tammany police justice named John M. Bloodgood made it a practice to pass through the poor neighborhoods with a large basket filled with pies and cakes and meat. Later it was learned that the money to pay for such things came from money extorted by the Honorable Mr. Bloodgood from the counterfeiters and prostitutes who came before him in court. But no one in the Sixth Ward was shocked by this. They thought it rather clever.

Still there was need for a gesture—a single incident to show the city that the huge army of the unwashed, ill-begotten carriers of bricks and the diggers of ditches had a voice and a very loud one.

The issue, when it came, was an improbable one. One might have thought that Rynders would have rallied his forces behind agitation for better housing, perhaps, or cheaper flour. But the issue involved "Patriotism" with overtones of "Art." Which are better, the burning question ran, American or English actors? And the Sixth Ward gangsters were ranged, down to the last brass knuckle, on the side of America.

In the late 1840's, a feud developed between Edwin Forrest, the country's most popular actor, and William C. Macready, a very popular English actor. And when, in the spring of 1849, it was discovered that they would both be appearing in *Macbeth* at the same time and in the same city, what had been mere professional rivalry quickly flowered into personal and mutual dislike.

Somehow the news of this rather esoteric rivalry traveled down to the Bowery and came to the ears of Captain Rynders. It is a tribute to his astuteness that he saw in this remote, academic dispute a battle cry and a standard. There were attenuating circumstances. Forrest was practically a neighborhood boy. He had started his career in a Bowery theater and, while relations between the Five Pointers and the Bowery Boys were frequently cool, still there was a feeling of neighborliness where the uptown folks were concerned. And Macready. An Englishman! It was perfect. Many of the Sixth Ward boys still spoke with the brogue of the old country, and "Englishman" was a fighting word. Rynders rose to the occasion. If these people followed him into battle, all the more certain that they would follow him to the polls. On this simple concept, Napoleon had built an empire. Rynders would try the same. Handbills and posters appeared suddenly in public places asking if Englishmen were to be allowed to run the country.

The arrival of a British ship in the harbor was propitious. Suddenly new posters appeared throughout the East Side probably written by Rynders himself:

"Workmen, shall Americans or Englishmen rule in this city? The crew of the British steamer have threatened all Americans who shall dare to express their opinion this night at the English Aristocratic Opera House! We advocate no violence, but a free expression of opinion to all public men. Washington forever! Stand by your lawful rights!" It was signed "American Committee."

Soldiers of the Sixth Ward, three decades of inexperience looked down upon you. On the evening of May 7, 1849, a ragged army swarmed out of the Five Points and the Bowery and marched uptown to the Astor Place Opera House, an imposing Romanesque building of many columns which stood on the corner of Eighth and Layfayette Streets. The mob was disorganized, but coming up the street it had a certain compelling look and the ticket taker was not so foolish as to try to bar it. Macready was driven from the stage. He slipped out a side door and returned to his hotel. These

Americans! They can't read—half of them, but each one is a critic!

There was high revel that night in the saloons of the Bowery and the sad little dance halls of the Five Points. But the more conservative people of the city were shocked and angered. They suspected who was at the bottom of all this. That Tammany leader down in the Bowery. Must we surrender everything to him and his ruffian followers?

A delegation waited upon Mr. Macready. Would he be so kind as to try again? This time there would be protection. Macready pondered awhile and announced that he would return that night to the same stage.

The Sixth Warders were shocked at the news. This was open defiance. It was a challenge to their wickedness—the only art they knew. It had to be avenged.

And it was.

May 10, 1849. Police estimated that the mob that swarmed into the open area before the theater numbered ten to fifteen thousand. Many of the mobsters had tickets. Rynders thought of everything. They crowded into the theater and waited for the curtain to rise.

The curtain was late. Backstage, Macready was advised that he had better not go on. He looked through the little hole in the curtain trying to see if friends outnumbered enemies. There were cheers alternating with the groans and whistles. He was not afraid of the mob, and he would not disappoint his friends.

"Raise the curtain," he said.

And the curtain went up.

FIRST WITCH: "When shall we three meet again
                In thunder, lightning or in rain?"

SECOND WITCH: "When the hurlyburly's done,
                When the battle's lost and won."

The audience was strangely silent. Macready did not appear until the third scene and the Bowery Boys and Five Pointers wanted it to be clear whom it was they were protesting against. There were cheers for the witches and Duncan. It looked like maybe the evening would go well after all.

DUNCAN: "No more that thane of Cawdor shall deceive
Our bosom interest:-go pronounce his present death,
And with his former title greet Macbeth."

ROSS: "I'll see it done."

DUNCAN: "What he hath lost noble Macbeth hath won."

Great cheers and applause. More than the scene deserved. But they were waiting. Everyone there was waiting.

Act I, Scene iii, *A Heath. Enter Macbeth and Banquo.*

MACBETH: "So foul and fair a day I have not seen."

He threw the line at them. It was a gauntlet thrown down to the mob, and a gracious thank you to those who were his friends.

THIRD WITCH: "All hail, Macbeth, thou shalt be king hereafter!"

Not that night he wouldn't. The groans and catcalls welled up from the darkness of the orchestra and balconies. Then there was a rain of rotten fruit squashing down on the stage and beating against the scenery. The actors' lines were drowned out for the most part but some came through and brought applause.

BANQUO: "If you can look into the seeds of time,
And say which grain will grow and which will not,

Speak, then, to me, who neither beg nor fear
Your favors nor your hate."

Someone ripped up a chair and threw it onto the stage. It crashed at the actors' feet and lay there like some grotesque, distorted symbol of the evening's doings.

Outside, thousands who had not been able to gain entrance milled around. Then someone shouted an order. It was Rynders, probably. A shower of bricks and cobblestones beat against the theater front. Police managed to arrest a few of the rioters and to lock them up in the theater basement. But the Sixth Ward bred sturdy men. They promptly set the building on fire.

Inside, the manager held up a sign to the audience: "The friends of order will remain quiet." But it was too late. The mobsters had won. Macready finally shrugged and with the rest of the cast walked off the stage. In the general confusion that followed, he mingled with the crowd, walked out a side entrance, escaped and made plans to return to a realm secure against the envy of less happy lands.

But the mob lingered long after he had fled, calling upon him (with the illogic of all mobs) to come forth and be hanged.

The police were helpless in the face of such numbers and the Seventh Regiment was summoned and marched double time down the street. And, as with all the diversions of the Bloody Auld Sixth, the burlesque turned to tragedy. The troops were met by a howling mass of men and women who tossed stones into their stiff ranks. The order was given to halt and shoulder arms.

"Blanks!" someone shouted. "Their guns are loaded with blanks."

The guardsmen fired. Thirty-seven of the rioters and bystanders were killed and as many injured.

The evening was over. Captain Rynders survived, of course.

Police later determined that the inflammatory handbills that had been posted throughout the lower city had been delivered to a saloon across the street from City Hall. Rynders had his Empire Club upstairs. But that was as close as they got. Rynders denied all charges, grew in stature and influence in Tammany and eventually saw himself ranged on the side of law and order as a United States marshal. It took a special breed of men to achieve success in the city's politics in that time of change. The rules were not yet laid down. No one was quite sure where shrewdness ended and dishonesty began. And the most successful of all were those who simply wrote their own rules . . .

When Bill Tweed was thirteen he went to work as an errand boy and apprentice in the shop of Isaac Fryer, a saddler and dealer in hardware. Then, after a year, he had his last brush with education. It was a rather good one. He was sent to the boarding school of the Reverend John Taylor Halsey, an aristocrat of stern Presbyterian morality and the son of a man who had helped found the Society of the Cincinnati and who had known Washington and Lafayette. Many of the students were sons of well-to-do families. Tweed stayed there a year. We can only guess as to his response to the company of his classmates. When he returned home a year later, he had had enough of education. And he had no difficulty taking up his role as the most promising young man in the neighborhood. He was fifteen now. Not quite a man yet. But no longer a boy.

The Reverend Mr. Halsey had done his best with his tall, stocky, articulate and rather intense student from New York. Tweed at least knew figures. He knew them well enough to get a job as a junior clerk with the J. and G. C. Alexander Company, a tobacco firm on Front Street. By nineteen, he was a member of the firm.

His father, meanwhile, had been doing well. He had

bought part interest in a brush factory on Pearl Street. The principal owner was an old friend of the family named Joseph C. Skaden.

Young Tweed found himself frequently going to the Skaden house for advice on all sorts of things. Skaden had taken a fondness to Tweed and a friendship developed between the older man and the brash young man. And the Skaden house was congenial for another reason. There was Mary Jane Skaden. She was eighteen in 1844, the year Tweed became twenty-one. Young Tweed had frequently conferred with Skaden about personal decisions. Now, the most personal decision of all. Mary Jane and I, Sir . . . well, while I have valued your friendship for many years, it has not been because of that alone that I came so frequently to this house. You see, Sir . . .

Skaden was delighted. Tweed and Mary Jane were married in St. Stephen's Episcopal Church on the corner of Chrystie and Broome Streets. The Reverend Joseph H. Prince performed the ceremony. Tweed and his young bride took up residence at his father-in-law's house at 193 Madison Street. It was less than half a mile from Number One Cherry Street. He would see the same people that he had seen almost every day of his life. And he would walk the same streets.

But he was growing restless and anxious to meet his destiny.

The neighborhood needed a new fire company. An earlier one, the "Black Joke" company, had been disbanded. On December 11, 1848, there was a meeting in Andrew Maner's ink factory on Gouverneur Street near Monroe. The proposal was advanced that a new fire company be established. It had been talked about for months. And now it was time for action. The preliminaries had been taken care of . . . Shall we then, gentlemen, proceed? It was duly proposed and voted. And William Marcy Tweed was, of course, a member.

There are moments in the lives of individuals when the future seems to make itself manifest. This was one of them— Bill Tweed helping to establish a fire company. That meant even more fame in the neighborhood. It would mean that he would meet more people and be seen by more. It would mean that his name would be mentioned occasionally in the newspapers. Ward leaders were constantly on the lookout for such as these. And they would hear about Big Bill . . .

Two weeks later the group met over a beer saloon on Hester Street. What should be the name of the new company? Black Joke was a logical choice, but that name had bad connotations. Too much fighting. "Fredonia"? "Eureka"? Both were voted down. Tweed took the floor. Why not name the company after the man who was so closely identified with the discovery of America? Americus Vespucci? From the distance of over a hundred years, this doesn't seem to have been such a compelling suggestion, but perhaps we underestimate the persuasive qualities of the good-looking, brown-haired, flint-eyed Tweed. At any event, his suggestion was accepted and voted on and that night there came into being the "Americus Engine Company No. 6."

What about a symbol? Tweed supplied this, too. A tiger. Tweed liked that. It was ferocious-looking and the very symbol of power and cunning. Someone painted a tiger's head on the box of the engine. It was a splendid painting. The tiger's face was distorted into a snarl. You could see the teeth. Tweed loved to look at it as he and the other volunteer firemen trotted along with the engine. No one takes liberties with a tiger. This city—it's not unlike a jungle. It's good when other animals get out of your way. Tweed loved that picture.

Coincidently young Thomas Nast, down at the school in Chrystie Street, had also been intrigued by a picture of a tiger. There was one in a printed sign pasted on a wall he passed on his way to school. One day, when he thought no one was looking, he ripped it off and stuffed it quickly into his jacket. But not quickly enough. A member of the city watch had seen him and young Nast, scurrying home, was surprised and shocked to have a club suddenly slammed down on his behind.

The watchman took the poster away from him. Beautiful print, it was. A tiger's face distorted into a snarl. Nast was devastated by the loss. Where would he ever see such a picture again?

In later years the young artist remembered another incident that happened about that time. He was walking along one of the neighborhood streets one day when suddenly a young boy jumped at him from a doorway and let go with a shattering blast from a toy fireman's trumpet. Nast ran in terror at the sound and the fierce aspect of the boy. Years later he would remember the incident quite clearly. The boy, he recalled, was dressed in the uniform of a volunteer fireman . . .

Tweed, with his harsh good humor and gross joviality, found expression and congeniality among the other volunteers. By July, he was assistant foreman. And the following summer he was elected foreman. A few weeks after his election, the seventy-five other members of the fire company presented him with a watch. It was engraved "To William Marcy Tweed from the members of the Americus Engine Company No. 6." He would wear it all his life. William Marcy Tweed, foreman of Americus Engine Company No. 6. Suddenly he was somebody. He had a title and people remembered his name. Big Bill Tweed. He had a ready grin and a warm handshake. Everybody liked Big Bill. And his name came up at a meeting in Tammany Hall.

The year he became foreman of the Big Six, Tweed was nominated for assistant alderman. The city's legislative body in 1849 was called the Common Council. It was divided into aldermen and assistant aldermen, twenty of each.

Tweed didn't campaign very hard. The Seventh Ward where he lived was fairly evenly divided between Whig and Democrat, but Tweed was sure he had it wrapped up. His opponent was a man named Thomas Woodward, a quiet-spoken, efficient person, but who'd ever heard of him? Tweed shook some hands, smiled a lot, and spent most of his time with his friends at the fire house. They were sure he'd win. Everyone knew Big Bill Tweed. And everybody liked him. Fine man, Tweed . . .

When the votes were counted, Tweed got a shock. The vote was 1,428 for Woodward; 1,381 for Tweed. He had lost by forty-seven votes. Not bad for a young man his first time out.

But Tweed was shocked. There were 1,428 voters in the Seventh Ward who had voted against him. He had run and lost. It really hurt. Leadership had always been his. The Cherry Hillers had known that . . . the boys of the Big Six . . . everybody except 1,428 Whig-voting Seventh Ward people.

Tweed pretended unconcern. And his popularity in the ward was unabated. The Big Six was getting famous, and not only in New York but throughout the East. They received invitations to visit and meet with other volunteer firemen in other cities. This suited Tweed fine, and with funds donated by Tweed and his friends, the company started off on a junket. They visited Philadelphia, Baltimore and Washington. They paraded up Pennsylvania Avenue and later met President Millard Fillmore. They put on exhibitions of firefighting in Montreal and Quebec and finally came home. The Big Six was famous, and the members wore the figure 6 on their suspenders like a medal. Talk of the last election had pretty well died out. And no one seemed to remember. But Tweed remembered, and the hurt was there. He had really wanted to be assistant alderman. And he could hear ancestral voices: *I guess Thomas Ash was a pretty big man, Son. Your grandfather shod his horses, you know. Got to know him pretty well. Ash went into politics. Became treasurer of Tammany after awhile. Your grandfather always liked him. I guess he figured I'd go into politics. But I don't know . . . all that speech-making and such . . .*

And 1,428 people right in this ward had voted against him—people he probably saw every day. Well, to hell with them!

In 1851, Tweed was nominated again. This time for alderman. His Whig opponent was formidable: John B. Webb, a prominent boat-builder and a man of substance. And he was well liked.

Tweed did some long, hard thinking. You have to make your own rules sometimes. Rynders—there was a shrewd man. Everyone knew who had those posters printed. And Rynders was doing all right.

Tweed found the solution. Webb wasn't the only well liked Whig in the Seventh Ward. There was Joel Blackmer, for example. And, despite different political views, he and Tweed were friends. Blackmer had a lot of friends in the Ward. He was principal of a girls' school. The parents knew him well. And they respected him.

Tweed induced Blackmer to run for alderman that year as an independent. Tweed's arguments must have been persuasive. Certainly they were false. But Blackmer ran and split the ticket. It's impossible to say now if he knew what he was doing. But Tweed was very sure what he was doing.

And he had still another trick. Rynders again, probably. Tweed had some posters of his own printed up saying harsh things about Webb. He held them until shortly before election and then distributed them throughout the Seventh Ward. Webb took an advertisement in the *Herald* to denounce them. But it was Election Day when his denial appeared and pretty late. Webb was angry. "A paper signed 'Taxpayer' and addressed to the people of the Seventh Ward is a tissue of base and malignant lies . . ."

No doubt it was. Tweed wasn't going to lose again this time. He couldn't understand losing. Anything was acceptable as long as you won.

I am persuaded, Sir, that you agree with me in thinking that any political advantage, however great, would be bought too dear if obtained by countenancing such calumnies on our opponents . . .

But all that was a long time ago.

November 4, 1851. Election day. Blustery weather and rain. Still the voters turned out in unusual force. There was some fighting in the election places, especially in the Nineteenth Ward. But that had been expected. Mayor Ambrose C. Kingsland published a warning in the papers offering a reward of one hundred dollars for the detection of any person voting or attempting to vote illegally. It was a gesture only. Both parties were doing it. And there is no mention of anyone ever collecting that hundred dollars.

Rain and unusually high winds. New Yorkers were hoping that the weather would be pleasant for the anticipated visit of Louis Kossuth, the great Hungarian liberal and revolutionary. In 1851, "revolution" was still a pleasant word in New York.

An advertisement in the *Herald* that morning:

"Kossuth is coming. Ladies prepare.
Set your parlors to right with the greatest of care.
To polish your furniture without trouble or loss,
Make a trial of E. Parker's beautiful gloss."

It cost twenty-five cents a bottle. At Tripler Hall that night a singer named Catherine Hayes gave a concert, but it was ill-attended and the audience was not as enthusiastic as usual. She sang "Robert, Toi que j'aime," with only modest success, but did better later with a song called, "Are You Sure the News is True?"

The rain continued into the night. There was a big rally at Tammany Hall. Rynders was there and he made a speech. The reporter for the newly formed *New York Daily Times* left early to get the story in the next morning's edition. It would be the forty-fourth edition of the paper. It had appeared first on September 18th of that year, born in pain and travail in a little unfinished office building down at 113 Nassau Street. There were missing windows in the building. Type was set by candlelight. But Henry J. Raymond, editor, and his assistant, George Jones, dreamed big dreams. We will, they promised, "allay rather than excite agitation, and substitute reason for prejudice in all discussions of public affairs."

And so they did. It wasn't until later that *The Times* would get quite excited and do what it could to stir up agitation. Jones worked by candlelight that night. And the day would come when he would be offered three million dollars just to lay off. "You could live like a prince," they would tell him. But all that was decades ahead and on that night, Tweed was just a young man running for alderman on the Tammany ticket for the Seventh Ward.

Tweed won. He barely won. Blackmer had taken 206 Whig votes from Webb: 1,336 had voted for Webb: Tweed got 1,384. By inducing Blackmer to run, he had managed to squeeze out a plurality of forty-eight. And he was now an alderman-elect.

An alderman was an important man. He appointed the police of his ward. He granted, or withheld, licenses to saloons. He sat as a justice in the mayor's court which, Tweed was delighted to note, tried all cases of voting frauds. And with his fellows, he awarded valuable franchises to omnibus and ferry lines. Aldermen bought land for the city and determined the price therefor. And they could, with a little persuasion, determine who sat on the Grand Jury.

Tweed shook a lot of hands that night. He had won again. It was the Cherry Hillers all over again. You have to be shrewd. You have to be smart.

It was 1851. Edward Livingston had been dead for sixteen years. And the city had changed since his day. It was only the very old who remembered him at all.

CHAPTER 3

REHEARSAL FOR CORRUPTION

"We have been placed here as the representatives and guardians of the Empire City of the Union, to protect its great and increasing interests; and it becomes us to have a proper conception of the important trust confided in us. We must remember that although our course may soon run in this world, yet our acts will be recorded and they will perhaps be scrutinized by future generations."
— Richard T. Compton, President of the New York Board of Aldermen, in an address to the newly elected aldermen, January, 1852.

THEY APPLAUDED THAT, those who had been elected to sit there. Tweed applauded. He was twenty-eight now and already too fat. He looked like a greedy politician. His waistline was too big. When he had been foreman of the Big Six, the exercise had hardened his muscles and kept him reasonably trim. But not any more. He was eating too much. And on that January day he took his seat in the Common Council almost like a hungry man who sits down to a promised feast. He stood with the other aldermen and registered an oath to support the federal and state constitutions and the city ordinances. He signed his name in the register and noted his address—31 Rutgers Street. His place of business was Franklin Square. Richard T. Compton was elected President of the Board of

52

Aldermen. Tweed was appointed teller. Almost time for lunch.

But Compton is talking again: "We are the treasurers of the people . . ."

Tweed is a little uncomfortable in his new suit. It was after one o'clock and the weak winter sun was beginning to slant shadows across the common in front of City Hall. Why do some people have to make pompous speeches whenever they get a chance? Doesn't he know that no one is really listening?

". . . and by an economy in the use of their property we can best testify our appreciation of the honor they have conferred upon us. Failing in this we may all be assured that we will be held to a strict accountability for the misuse of the power vested in us."

He was through. There was applause again and a slow moving toward the doors. Strict accountability? That depends on how you keep your books. The assistant aldermen had adjourned, too. Twenty aldermen and twenty assistant aldermen filling the corridors of City Hall. Talk and cigar smoke.

They're not a bad-looking group of men. There's a sprinkling of lawyers. Compton, the president, is an ice merchant. Jacob T. Oakley is a liquor dealer. There are a number of liquor dealers. Alderman A. A. Alvord is an insurance broker.

It's 1852 and their potential for good or evil is enormous. The city is getting bigger every day. There is much to be done, and their predecessors were incompetent. There are slums to be attended to. Cheap saloons dot the city. "Porter houses," they are called by the people who own them. Down in the Bowery and the Five Points, thousands of homeless children roam the streets, selling papers or collecting rags. Girls, barefoot even in winter, sell ears of hot corn for a few pennies. And many of them, scarcely in their teens, offer other attractions at little advance in price. Immigrant ships arrive daily now and thousands more are pouring into the city. Bad pavements. In the winter, mud cakes the streets and in the summer, it's dust. Traffic is deplorable and for the very young or the very old, very dangerous. Cattle are driven through the streets to the slaughter houses downtown. New York is growing up and there is much to be done.

There was a need for giants. There was a need for men who could show the country and the world that representative, democratic government is a shining, splendid instrument. Europe had its ghettos and its legions of the thwarted and the hopeless. But Europe was old, and America was young. New York was young . . .

Compton . . . Oakley . . . Alvord . . . Tweed . . . They mill around. There's talk and cigar smoke and everyone is shaking hands. They would be known to history as "The Forty Thieves."

There was snow on the city streets that January Monday and Horace Greeley over at the *Tribune* had some harsh things to say about the slowness of the city in cleaning the walks in City Hall Park. In the Court of General Sessions, an eighteen-year-old boy named George W. Twibill pleads guilty to forging two orders for payments of ten and three dollars and is sentenced to two years in state prison. And "Ellen Russell, a female whose name is said not to be above reproach," is charged with stealing a gold watch and is held for trial. On Friday, Alderman Tweed holds an inquest on the body of one Jeremiah Dooley who had died the previous Monday after falling down a flight of stairs at 222 Stanton Street. It was an accident. There is talk of a law prohibiting the driving of cattle through the city streets . . .

And the tragedy, when it comes, begins as comedy.

On the last meeting in January, the aldermen voted themselves a tea room. *Resolved,* That the keeper of the City Hall be directed to furnish refreshments to the members of the Common Council whenever they meet in session, and that

the Comptroller be and is hereby authorized to pay all bills
for the same when duly certified on oath by said keeper.

It was an innocent enough beginning. A late supper for
the honorable gentlemen after they had been working late.
Surely no one could object to that.

Horace Greeley could. And did. The first bill was submitted to the comptroller on February 12th. It was duly
attested and witnessed by the new alderman from the Seventh
Ward, William M. Tweed. Mr. Greeley was shocked. The
Board had consumed 312½ pounds of beef at a cost of $46.80.
Sixty-one pair of chickens had cost the city $29.89. Oysters
are always nice after a hard day's work. The aldermen had
eaten $197.07 worth. Four thousand cigars; 176 eggs; 146
loaves of bread; 93 pounds of ham; 50 pounds of sausage; 95
pounds of butter; and 16 pair of quail. Furthermore, the tea
room had been voted on the very last session of the month,
and so the items listed must all have been consumed at that
final session. To charge for previous meals would have been
illegal.

Greeley did a little arithmetic. His figures were unassailable. On the night in question, each alderman and assistant
alderman had eaten 8 pounds of beef, 1½ chickens, 225
oysters, 40 eggs, 3½ loaves of bread, 2 pounds of ham and a
pound of sausage. And each of them had smoked 100 cigars.

It wasn't much of a steal, perhaps. But it was a beginning.
The city needed land for a potter's field. There were sixty-
nine acres available on Ward's Island in the East River. The
plot was worth perhaps $30,000 at most. The aldermen
bought it for $103,450 . . .

Tweed was learning. By early summer, he and the others
had appropriated $4,100 for fireworks to be displayed on
the Fourth of July. They were worth no more than $500. As
with the potter's field purchase, the difference was split
among those who helped push the measure through. And

one of those who must have taken his cut was the Mayor, Ambrose C. Kingsland, a Whig.

The news came June 30th that Henry Clay, the distinguished senator from Kentucky, had died in Washington. He was a Whig, true, but the Democratic aldermen were determined that the city should do its part in observing the obsequies. The body must be brought to City Hall to lie in state. And there will have to be crepe, of course, for the front of the building. A delegation should be on the boat that takes the body to Albany. It'll have to be fed—$3,900 should take care of everything. It wouldn't be commensurate with the dignity of this great city to do anything less.

Some of the newspapers were getting restive. Was $3,900 necessary, really? It was a fortune. Could it be that some of the honorable gentlemen were being careless with the city's money? Could it be that such appropriations were financially profitable to them?

It was the time to stop. And there were some of them who knew it. Over in the Board of Assistant Aldermen, one of them takes the floor to counsel caution. "Let the Board pause," he says, "in what they are doing."

To Tweed that was dangerous talk. It was almost as though he realized that his destiny was being challenged. And, as always when someone advanced a suggestion he did not approve, he felt that it was a personal affront. His response that day was the same as when he had bossed the Cherry Hillers and someone objected to his leadership. He fought back. He fought back harder than was necessary.

On July 12th, the Board of Aldermen adopted a resolution challenging the press to show fraud. It was an audacious move. But its very presumption was in its favor. And it worked. The newspapers did not accept the challenge. They could not at that time prove a single bribe. They had no facts to sustain an indictment. Tweed had risked that. He

couldn't have been sure. He rose at a meeting of the board
to exult in the victory. Newspaper reporters, he said, take
bribes to advance the interests of the rich.

"We know the virtue of a fifty dollar bill when it is wisely
employed, and the echo it will produce."

Audacity. Hit the enemy hard. Keep him on the defensive
and you never have to defend yourself. The newspapers are
tools of the rich, he says, and he will not surrender to them.
"Their noise is of little importance. There is not one of
them scarcely worth reading, and most of them are never
read at all."

He was wrong. But it would take a long time to prove that.
The potter's field steal . . . that appropriation for fireworks
and the crepe for Clay's funeral . . . it had been incredibly
easy.

If he felt any emotion at all at the turn of events, it was
probably one of sheer surprise. It was all so easy. Most people
are sheep. They're afraid. They're afraid of newspapers.
They're afraid of the law. They're afraid of God. Tweed
wasn't afraid of anyone.

*I guess Thomas Ash was a pretty big man, Son. Your
grandfather shod his horses, you know. Got to know him
pretty well. Ash went into politics . . .*

That didn't bother him either. He was a politician now
and the craft wasn't like his grandfather had thought it was.
Honor and dignity? Well, his grandfather had died poor.
And Big Bill Tweed was getting rich. The first Tweed who
ever did. And it was easy. It was all so easy. And everybody
liked him. The people of the Seventh Ward certainly did.
And he was getting known around in other wards, too. Some
pretty important men at Tammany Hall went out of their
way to talk with him and shake his hand. It was probably
the same in Albany or even Washington.

The Congress of the United States! Just like in the Common Council but on a bigger scale. Congressman William Marcy Tweed. It had a good sound. Well, why not? It might just be that future generations would know his name. William Marcy Tweed, a poor chairmaker's son who rose to the top.

That summer the Board of Aldermen paid out $600,000 for a paving job on the Bowery that was so badly done that it all had to be ripped up shortly after. The newspapers made a lot of that. But, again, they couldn't prove anything. Furthermore, an attack on Tweed and the other Forty Thieves was getting to be expensive. Every year the city bought thousands of dollars of newspaper space for public notices. These were quietly withdrawn from unfriendly papers and placed with editors who had a more sympathetic attitude. "The satanic press," Greeley called it. But he probably had to justify the loss of income to the *Tribune* owners nevertheless. It was so easy . . .

Tweed decided to run for Congress at the next election. William Marcy Tweed, statesman. Not bad for a chairmaker's son.

But perhaps the elder Tweed was beginning to have doubts about his jovial, hand-shaking son. The brush business Richard Tweed had with Skaden had been a helpful addition to his income. But basically he was a maker of chairs. All this talk of politics. He had heard it often before. But maybe the measure of a man can be taken in other ways. Perhaps one way is to watch him at his craft and see the things he has made with his own hands.

So Richard had taken Big Bill and his brother, Young Richard, into partnership. Politics is fine, but the best thing you can leave your sons is a well-paying business. Richard was growing old and tired. How lucky he was to have sons to carry on.

But one son gambled too much and the other gave most

of his time to the demands of ward politics. And the business failed.

Bill Tweed didn't care, of course. He had found a more efficient way of making money. Then one day his father asked for an accounting. Bill Tweed was a little hurt. For months he had given his father an allotment, calling it his part of the profits. But the time had come to tell the truth. There were no profits. Politics takes time. The business was bankrupt.

The old man nodded and turned away. All those years of work. The fever had come and still he had stayed and attended to his business. Some people said that a Tweed-made chair was the best chair in the city.

Tweed could never understand it. He felt hurt and confused. But he didn't really comprehend. That grimy, stinking chair factory. Could his father really feel pride in that? He had been getting a monthly payment. What difference did it make where it came from?

Tweed would never really know. You won or you lost. Too bad the old man was one of the losers . . .

And there were others. It was almost as if he carried an infection without himself showing the symptoms. And again, he was surprised at how it all came out.

For some time there had been talk of building a street railway along Broadway. It was a good idea. Horsecars would be a considerable improvement over the unreliable omnibuses that crowded the street and threw mud over the sidewalks. There would be a schedule. The cars would run on rails and the ride would be smoother. Bids were open. It was Christmas time and it would be the last piece of business for the year.

One of the bidders who approached the honorable aldermen was a shrewd and practical gentleman with the Dickensian name of Jacob Sharp. He proposed to build a street railway from South Ferry to Fifty-ninth Street. There were four other bidders, one offering to give the city one cent out of each five cents collected in fares. Sharp offered no such inducement. Instead, he had a confidential talk with Tweed. Across more than a century you can almost hear the money being counted out.

The Board of Aldermen passed a resolution granting Sharp the franchise. The bill went to the Mayor for his signature. Work would begin shortly after New Year's. God rest ye, merry gentlemen.

But there was an unexpected hitch. Alexander T. Stewart, owner of Stewart's huge department store at Broadway and Chambers Street, turned livid at the news. Horsecars on Broadway! Most of his customers arrived in carriages. This would ruin business!

Stewart was not one to give bribes. But he was a powerful man and when he spoke people listened. Even mayors. Stewart advised Mayor Kingsland that the franchise was a steal. There was bribery in the Common Council. The measure must be vetoed.

Mayor Kingsland was impressed. First the newspapers and now Stewart. It was enough. To hell with Tweed. And when the measure came to his desk, he vetoed it.

The news was brought to Tweed. And once again he was in a fight. He pretended anger but he probably was enjoying the whole thing. It was simple. At his bidding, the Board would pass the measure over the Mayor's veto.

But Tweed was up against a real antagonist this time. Stewart was worth probably ten million dollars and he wasn't afraid to fight. An alderman take on Stewart? Only Tweed would have dared. But he did. The Cherry Hillers—Webb— the newspapers. One more enemy to challenge his right to rule. It was the old story. But this time he was in Big Time.

Stewart went to court and obtained an injunction enjoining the Board from taking further action on the measure. And it was duly served on the Board. They could still override the Mayor's veto but that would be contempt of court. They could go to jail.

Most of the aldermen had had enough of the fight. You can't contest with ten million dollars. Give Sharp his money back if we have to. It's better than going to jail.

Sheep. Afraid of the law, all of them. Afraid of what God might do. Afraid of Alexander T. Stewart, a Broadway shopkeeper!

But not all were afraid. And Tweed found support from an unexpected source. It was a fellow alderman standing upon principle. Tweed was a little shocked, but when you're in a fight you take help where you can find it.

Alderman Oscar W. Sturtevant was a young lawyer who had been elected to the Common Council at the same time as Tweed. Sturtevant had been a poor boy, success had not come easily, and the struggle had left him with an almost aggressive attachment to "the people." He had a rather boring way of asserting whenever it was even remotely germane that he had been born among the people and would die among them. And, although he was doing well, he seemed to revel in stories of his poverty. Now Stewart, a millionaire, was trying to thwart the will of the duly elected representatives of the people. He and Tweed had a long talk about the injunction. Sturtevant thought it a gross intrusion by the court into the affairs of a legislative body. Tweed agreed. Sturtevant nursed his wrath. The courts have always been the last resort of special privileges. Tweed found this pretty shocking, he said. And he blew on the coals. Stewart, he pointed out, was a rich man. Lived uptown. Well, there's no use trying to fight ten million dollars. The people have lost again, I guess.

Not so. Sturtevant vowed that so long as he was a member

of the Common Council no lackey judge was going to thwart
his will. And he drew up a document to be read in the Common Council the next day.

He wrote well. And what he wrote was true. Tweed was
delighted. This business of ethics . . . it's a great argument.
It's like having the Church on your side, or George Washington.

The next day the aldermen listened closely while the clerk
read Sturtevant's resolution: "If the assumption be submitted
to, that a Judge, without color of law or jurisdiction can
exercise the prerogative of directing and controlling municipal legislation of the City by issuing an injunction prohibiting the Mayor, Aldermen and Commonalty of New York
from performing a legislative act supposed by him to be
probably about to be performed, the next natural step of
jurisdictional usurpation will be to arrest and veto, in
similar manner, the legislation of the State, or that of Congress on any Judge's opinion of Constitutionality, expediency,
or motive . . ."

It was a good argument. And it still is. But some aldermen
held back. A troubled conscience always counsels caution.
This talk of bribes from the court. It would be unfortunate
if that were explored too closely.

Sturtevant had an answer: "The Common Council have
an equal authority to suspect and impute improper motives
to any intended judicial decision of any judge, and conse-
quently arrest his action on the bench, as such judge has in
regard to the legislative action of the Common Council."

As soon as the reading was done, Tweed leaped to his feet
to second it. And it was carried.

But would the Council vote to override the Mayor's veto?

Sturtevant takes the floor: "Now, I have known the Chief
Magistrate of this city long and intimately. I have known
him for twenty years and I have the highest respect for him.

He was like myself. We began the world two poor boys with very little in either of our breeches' pockets. He is, as I am myself, one of the people . . ."

Tweed didn't want to hear the rest. Neither did anyone else. Sturtevant had served his purpose. And a vote was called for.

The Mayor's veto was overridden by fifteen to three. Two of the aldermen did not commit themselves.

The court was not amused. And it moved with uncharacteristic speed. The whole Board of Aldermen was summoned to appear and show cause why they should not be held in contempt.

Tweed was almost arrogant as he took his seat. Send the whole Board of Aldermen to jail? They wouldn't dare.

They didn't. The aldermen who had voted against granting the franchise were fined two hundred dollars. The others were fined three hundred and fifty dollars.

Tweed almost laughed. Three hundred and fifty dollars! That might have been big money to his father, but it was nothing to him. Audacious. You have to be audacious . . .

But there was more. In the matter of Oscar W. Sturtevant, author of the resolution counseling defiance of the injunction: Alderman Sturtevant is himself an attorney and hence conversant with the law. It is deplorable that one of his experience should feel compelled to obviate the machinery whereby the courts sustain an order. Such conduct is not to be easily excused . . .

Sturtevant flushes slightly. Then the sentence. A fine of three hundred and fifty dollars and confinement in City Prison for fifteen days.

Prison! Alderman Sturtevant made a courtly bow to the bench as the judge finished. But in those brief moments his world had ended and things would never be the same. The years of study . . . all the people who had faith in him.

Prison! Fifteen days! He had often wondered how a man felt when he was sentenced to a jail cell. The curious impersonality of the processing period. The way they speak of you in your presence as though you cannot hear or cannot be trusted to make a proper response. Has this man had breakfast, Sheriff . . .

Tweed watched, curiously detached, as Sturtevant sat down again. Sturtevant's face was white now. He picks up a paper and his hand is shaking.

Oscar W. Sturtevant, man of the people. Well, he'd find quite a few people where he was going. Too bad. Oscar W. Sturtevant, lawyer and alderman, and now he had to go to jail.

Sturtevant and his father, Richard. They were strangely alike. At times their expression was even the same. Ethics— dedication to ideals . . .

Too bad. Some people win and some people lose . . .

But the Forty Thieves are pressing their luck. Even the *Herald,* usually a champion of the aldermen, hits out at them: "Hitherto our Common Council have asserted that their acts could not be questioned. It is now to be tested whether they are amenable to the laws as well as other citizens."

Greeley joins in. His paper prints some damning figures. It's a comparison of expenses in the city for 1851 and the year just ended. In 1851, it cost $180,000 to clean the city streets. In one year the Forty Thieves ran that up to $290,000. Expenses for street lighting went from $185,000 to $270,000. The Fire Department cost the city $82,000 in 1851 and $110,000 in 1852. Police: $530,000 to $615,000. Street repairs were up from $131,000 to $285,000. And printing expenses for the city almost doubled: $45,000 to $70,000.

"Now what is the explanation of all this?" This is Greeley

writing, and Greeley when angry was a crusade all by himself: "How does it happen that this extraordinary increase
in the particulars has taken place? Here is an item of street
cleaning, for example, which was in 1851 but $180,000 now
carried to $290,000 or almost double the amount. Is the city
cleaner as a whole than in 1850? Is any part or locality less
filthy? And if not—and all must answer no improvement has
taken place—then where has the extra $110,000 gone? Who
has got it? In what way has the city government disposed of
it? What is their explanation? We know of none whatever."

It was not easy to answer Mr. Greeley. And the rumblings
grow louder. And not just from newspapers. It was wage
earners now—professional people, butchers, bakers.

Tammany Hall. They own the city, those fellows.

And what a city it was! The whole East Side, once a gentle,
gracious place, was rapidly becoming one huge slum. There's
a police chief who dines with gamblers and tips his hat to the
madams who are prompt with their weekly contributions.
There were 5,910 places where liquor was sold in the city and
most of them stayed open on Sundays. In the Sixth Ward
alone, there were 706 rum shops or about one saloon to
every two voters. One agency estimated that there were about
900 male adults in the ward who were illiterate. That was
a little embarrassing to Tammany because the Democratic
majority there one year was 989. The Five Points area of the
"Bloudy Old Sixth" was a festering place of mud and
violence, drunkenness and juvenile tuberculosis. There's a
temperance meeting on a street corner. A speaker who, he
declares, was once a victim of rum, relates the joys of ab-
stinence. Passersby are beguiled. In the Sixth Ward you
took entertainment as it came. Pamphlets are handed out to
the crowd and the meeting ends with a song, sung to the tune
of *"The Star-Spangled Banner"*

"What a blessing 'twould be
If all men were but free
From the reign of the tyrant that breeds but confusion.
If some angel of love could descend from above
Show the follies of rum and dispell its illusions.
Then farewell we should say to the terrible sway
Of the monster whom then we should cease to obey
For the banner of freedom should float on the breeze
And soberness spread o'er the land and the seas."

The saloon keepers usually encouraged such meetings. Free advertisement. Great for business.

Tammany was riding high. The leaders were powerful, arrogant and, occasionally, careless. They nominated a man named Gustav Heberman as civil justice of the District Court, and he was duly elected. Mr. Heberman was by trade a dealer in fish, and he had had no legal training. But he was quite touched at the confidence placed in him by the voters and on his first day in court had a brief comment for his many friends who had come to see good old Gus dressed up in a black robe. He banged the gavel for silence.

"In deepest gratitude for your confidence I can only recompense you by promising that while I have the honor of occupying this seat of justice I shall, in the discharge of my duties, be neither partial nor impartial."

Judge Heberman's decisions have not survived as models of legal wisdom. In the case of Brown versus Lane, he felt quite competent to render a decision despite the fact that everyone in the ward knew that he and Lane were old and dear friends. Brown's lawyer framed a question and Judge Heberman held it out of order. The attorney reworded it and tried again. Judge Heberman responded quickly. "Hold on, young man," he said. "You can go on and ask that question, but I bet you ten dollars, you'll lose your case."

People speak openly of graft in the Common Council. And one of their own members is indiscreet. It's Alderman Denman—Ashel A. Denman. In a confidential moment he tells of some of the backstage agreements in the Council. It's easy to get a favorable vote if you know how. And he mentions a figure: ten thousand.

It was careless of Alderman Denman to speak so freely of confidential matters. The February Grand Jury was nearing the end of its term. But there was time enough for an investigation. And witnesses were called.

The honorable gentlemen in the Common Council had been careless. It was quite possible for them to pack a grand jury with sympathetic jurors. But they had been so busy that no one had attended to this and—chilling thought!—honest men had been selected. It must never happen again. It may be too late already.

A Mr. Bryan whose relations with the aldermen is suspect is called before the jury and asked a question: "Did you ever offer a bribe to a member of the Common Council?"

Mr. Bryan searches his memory, looks quickly at his lawyer, and says nothing. The question is repeated. The jurors lean forward to hear the answer. Mr. Bryan refuses to answer.

Very well. Perhaps the same question asked by the judges of the Court of Sessions will make him change his mind. There he can be ordered to answer. If he refuses, he can go to jail. Think it over, Mr. Bryan.

The aldermen were really worried this time. The Court of Sessions! The witness will surely talk. The whole thing is going to blow up!

Tweed is worried, too. But a plan is forming. The February Grand Jury will terminate automatically at the end of the month. Bryan is scheduled to appear on the 25th. That's a Friday. If he could just get a delay of a few days . . .

The Court of Sessions was composed of three judges. A Judge Beebe was the presiding judge assisted by two others who were chosen from the Board of Aldermen. Normally they could be counted on to defend their fellow aldermen. But everybody was afraid now. Who wants to defy Greeley and James Gordon Bennett and those fellows on *The Times* and Stewart with his righteous ire and his ten million dollars. Even the public was getting angry.

When court convened that Friday, Tweed was sitting in the first row of the spectators' seats. Around and behind him were other members of the Common Council. Reporters compared notes to make sure they had all the names correctly. Something was up.

Something was. Tweed sat immobile like a sullen Buddha. He ignored the witness completely. And he never even glanced at Judge Beebe. He watched the other two judges. His eyes went with almost pendulum regularity from one to the other. It took the concurrence of two of the three judges to sustain a decision. Judge Beebe sat in the middle. On one side was Judge William J. Brisley, alderman and stone cutter. On the other side was John Doherty, lawyer. Tweed sat silently, his face impassive. And his eyes sought first one aldermanic judge and then the other. There were no threats. There were no words. His face was almost without expression. It was only his eyes that moved at all. But he seemed to fill the room.

Judge Beebe repeated the question: "Did you ever offer a bribe to a member of the Common Council?"

Mr. Bryan's lawyer interrupts. He has not had time, Your Honor, properly to prepare his case. Judge Beebe remarks that there is no case to be prepared. The witness has simply been asked a question.

Tweed in the front row. Even when the two aldermanic judges look away, they can feel his eyes on them. "Will the

witness answer the question?" He will not. There is a stir
in the courtroom. Bryan is obviously in contempt of court.
Judge Beebe confers with his two associates.

Tweed's eyes. They're almost closed. Two narrow slits . . .

Judge Beebe addresses the court. He is angry and his face
is a little flushed.

"My associates and I differ in opinion. They consider this
a very serious case and are inclined to grant counsel for Mr.
Bryan time to prepare his argument."

He does not have to answer.

The case will go back to the March Grand Jury. And there
are those who will see to it that the March Grand Jury is not
fired with civic zeal in the matter of bribes to aldermen.
Tweed will see to it.

It was close. Reporters move toward the door. So does
Tweed. It had been close.

Greeley again: "Do honest men unite in trained bands to
awe courts and frown down witnesses? Do honest judges
insist upon deciding questions in which they are personally
interested? If no bribe has been received (not merely offered)
how foolish of the Aldermen to smother a document from
the Grand Jury which would blow to the winds all the
charges of corruption, silence the thunders of the Press, and
establish the purity of the Common Council beyond the
reach of malice. If honest, why object to having it known?"

A young showman from Connecticut named Phineas T.
Barnum offers a new attraction in his museum of curiosities.
It's called "The Forty Thieves." It turns out to be about
Ali Baba, but some thought it was a pretty good joke.

But for many, it was no joke. It was all too much, even
for New York in 1853. The papers call for a mass meeting
at Metropolitan Hall for the night of March 5th. Seven-thirty
Friday night. All honest citizens interested in restoring decent government to our city will attend . . .

It was chilly that night and a little blustery. There were plenty of things to do in New York that night beside attending a mass meeting. At the Stuyvesant Institute at 659 Broadway, Professor Owen was going to lecture on spiritual manifestations and a "physical demonstration" from the other world was promised. *Twelfth Night* was at Burton's Theater on Chambers Street. *Everyone Has His Faults* was at Wallack's on Broadway. And a faintly scandalous farce was due at the new St. Charles Theater on the Bowery near Chatham Square. It was called, *The Double-Bedded Room*. *The Times,* very properly, makes no mention of it.

By six-thirty it was clear that there would be an overflow crowd. They came in droves. It was a quiet crowd. There were no placards. No angry words. No violence. It was an orderly crowd. But it was there. Over two hundred workers at the Webb Shipyard came in a delegation. They remember how it all started. Those lies about John B. Webb when he had run against Tweed. He was a good man and they liked him. They were there.

So were thousands of others. They fill the long rows of seats downstairs and then the upstairs tiers. There are standees at the back of the hall. And still they come. The street outside is filled with people. Word of what is going on inside is passed out to them by people standing in the doorway.

What is going on inside is simple. The Forty Thieves are being dishonorably discharged from their duties.

Peter Cooper is made chairman by acclamation. He is one of the most prominent businessmen in the city and his interests are universal. He owns a wire factory in Trenton, New Jersey, blast furnaces in Pennsylvania, a rolling mill and glue factory in New York City, foundries, iron mines. That year his Trenton factory would roll out the first structural iron for fireproof buildings. He is sixty-three and intensely interested in the future and well-being of New York City. He stands, acknowledges the applause and reads a little speech. The words are formal and strained. But it doesn't matter too much what he says. It means that, starting at that moment, the Forty could begin counting their days, almost their hours.

James W. Gerard, lawyer and philanthropist, is called to the speaker's stand. He is one of the founders of the "Society for the Reformation of Juvenile Delinquents." He is a dedicated public servant, sixty years old, a little garrulous:

"I behold before me a vast congregation of Kings. All you have to do is will the change . . . will it and you will have it. There is no iron despotism to grind you under its heels. There is no power on earth that can cripple your energies or trammel your will. All you have to do is by your little ballots to make a revolution more powerful than those gained at the cannon's mouth. There is your alternative, and there is your freedom."

There is a wave of applause. They can hear it on the street outside. Blocks away, passersby stop and listen. The echo would sound in the conference rooms at Tammany Hall downtown at Nassau and Frankfort Streets . . .

Henry J. Raymond, editor of *The Times,* is a speaker. His paper has promised to "allay rather than excite agitation, and to substitute reason for prejudice in all discussions of public affairs." He speaks the same way. There's a soft, round face, a dark mustache that blends in with his neatly clipped beard. He speaks to the point.

"The business of this meeting is not with the past but with the future. Leaving of whatever misconduct the past may have witnessed to the action of Grand Juries, of Courts of Law and of Public Opinion, our duty and our design here tonight are to prevent the recurrence of such evils in the years to come . . ."

And, unlike the other speakers, he has a plan. Elect a new Common Council of reform candidates. Take away the judicial functions of the aldermen. Abolish the useless Board of Assistants and add a greater number of aldermen. There is safety in numbers.

The meeting lasted until ten-thirty. And the next morning everyone spoke of reform. We need honest men in the Common Council . . .

The Forty Thieves had had their day. At the next election, most of them were returned to the obscurity whence they came. All except one, at least. Big Bill Tweed was elected to go to Congress. That smile—that handshake—Bill Tweed remembers your name . . .

But the story of the Forty Thieves was done.

Or almost so. Jacob Sharp didn't get his franchise, after all. The privilege of granting all street franchises was taken from the Common Council and lodged in the State Legislature.

Oscar Sturtevant was released from prison. The experience had changed him. No more talk about being one of the people. No more talk about ethics. He was disgraced in his own eyes. He still felt justified in the stand he had taken. Many lawyers had said they privately agreed. The other aldermen had agreed. Bill Tweed was with him all the way.

But it didn't matter any more. He was an ex-convict now. He was a felon. He avoided his old friends and his old haunts. He became secretive and alone. And one day, shortly after his release, Oscar Sturtevant, lawyer and public servant, collapsed in a hotel and died.

Tweed was probably sorry to hear the news. But he was Congressman William Marcy Tweed now, duly elected from the Fifth New York Congressional District. Let Cooper and the others talk reform until dawn if they wanted, they couldn't touch him. Congressman William Marcy Tweed.

It had been easy. Maybe the Senate will be next. *Senator and Mrs. William Marcy Tweed are cordially invited to attend a reception at the White House on Thursday next* . . .

Too bad about Sturtevant. He was weak, really. All that talk about ethics. Standing on a principle. Violation of the purpose of the law. "I was born among the people and I will die among them." And he hadn't even done that right. Death had caught him in the lobby of the Astor House, a synonym for wealth and exclusion.

Sturtevant and his ideals—Richard Tweed and his pride in those well-made chairs . . .

There were winners and there were losers. . . .

CHAPTER 4

BROWNSTONES AND BRICKBATS

"The People will elect me Mayor though I should commit a murder in my family between now and the election."
— Fernando Wood, Candidate for Mayor of New York City, 1854.

Washington was a small city in 1854, but it was too big for Congressman William Marcy Tweed. The very vocabulary was unfamiliar: "Will the Honorable Gentleman from North Carolina please explain precisely what he means by interests opposed to the tobacco trade? I have figures here which show undeniably that . . ." Congressman Tweed shifted uncomfortably in his chair. Tobacco trade? Are they going to spout about it all day? "Popular sovereignty"? . . . "Kansas-Nebraska Bill"? . . . What the hell kind of politics is this?

Nobody paid much attention to him except to ask support for a measure. No one talked about Tammany. Missouri Compromise they talked about—"Slavery must be contained" . . . "Did you read Senator Douglas' speech yesterday?"

Tweed hadn't and he didn't intend to. The Kansas-Nebraska Bill was passed. Tweed didn't give a damn. And out in Ripon, Wisconsin, a group of former Whigs, Free-Soilers

74

and anti-slavery Democracts got together to form a new
political party. The name "Republican" was suggested and
favorably received. Tweed didn't give a damn about that
either. Something about a lawyer from Springfield, Illinois.
Tells lots of jokes.

Tweed came home. And he would never go back. New
York was his home and he knew it now. The next year he got
himself elected to the City Board of Education. Not much
of a position for an ex-congressman, perhaps. But Tweed
knew what he was doing. It was the kind of politics that he
liked. Members of the Board of Education appointed the
teachers in the city schools. An appointment was a valuable
thing. And the value could be measured in real terms.

Years later an investigator would tell about those days:
"One poor little girl came upon the stand on crutches.
That lame girl was taxed $75 for a paltry situation of $300 a
year. I would ask, what could be more infamous? The man
who divides the earnings of a common prostitute is superior
to the man who would take blackmail for the position of a
teacher. It is the most astounding thing I ever heard of . . .
But we are told . . . that these things are organized all over
the city, and that everyone has his friends, and looks after
their interests."

Here was politics Tweed could understand. Easy as cutting
the tail off a pig. Tobacco trade? Kansas-Nebraska? Those
people talked and talked and not one of them made any
more money than a good saloon keeper.

*Senator and Mrs. William Marcy Tweed are cordially in-
vited to attend a reception at the White House Thursday
next . . .*

He had an answer to that, too.

"If I wanted to go to the Senate, I'd go: but what for? I
can't talk and I know it. As for spending my time hearing
a lot of snoozers discuss the tariff and the particulars of a

contract to carry the mails from Paducah to Schoharie, I don't think I'm doing that just now."

He wasn't. He was back in New York. Big Bill Tweed, leader of the Seventh Ward. Already they were saying that one day he'd run this town. And they were right.

And it was quite a town.

By 1856, New York had enveloped the stubbornly aristocratic Union Square area and had pushed beyond to Thirty-fourth Street. Red brick was losing favor as a building material and the drab monotony of brownstone was creeping through the side streets. There were about 630,000 persons living in New York City, most of them in their own homes. Slums had come to the once elegant little streets of the lower East Side, but apartment houses were as yet unknown. Harlem was a separate village, and beyond that there were only farms and country homes.

Most of the city streets were filthy and badly paved. Stages still rattled and rolled through Wall Street and Broadway, but they would soon give way to the more efficient horsecars that moved with relative ease on rails. Both would prove awkward for ladies who affected the hoop skirt which was just coming into style. Bleeker Street was the center of the city's Bohemian life, or, to use the contemporary phrase, the demi-monde.

A new song, "Melody in F," by Anton Rubenstein was becoming popular with the avant garde. Other New Yorkers were less critical. There was a song called "Twinkling Stars are Laughing, Love" which had great favor in the concert saloons, and young ladies who played the piano were kept busy learning new Stephen Foster songs. "Willie, We Have Missed You" was a popular one but would lose favor the next year to a song called "Come Into the Garden, Maud," music by Michael William Balfe to lyrics written by Alfred, Lord Tennyson.

Fashionable families around Washington Square were re-
sisting new and unsavory neighbors to the east, south and
west, and the St. John's Park area had gone into a decline
that would ultimately prove fatal. Since 1803, St. John's
Park had been the nucleus of one of the most fashionable
sections of town. It was on the west side of the city, a few
gracious, tree-shaded acres bounded by Varick, Beach, Hudson and Laight Streets, gas-lit by night and, by day, jealously
guarded by lovely old homes and nurses in uniforms and
their proper children. It was too gentle to survive the hungry
gnawings of the city and its very outlines now can scarcely
be traced. As of present writing, it's a parking lot for trucks.

Fifth Avenue was learning a new importance and becoming dotted with the homes of the newly rich who were putting up imposing, ornate, very expensive buildings, most of
them with a profusion of involved angles on the façade, high
windows and the inevitable trade entrance just below the
level of the street.

Broadway was busy and business-like, noisy, crowded and
important. And it was a social barometer of a sort. You could
tell a person's social standing quite accurately by watching
who nodded to him during a stroll down Broadway. Or, more
importantly, who did not.

The Bowery was the Broadway of the East Side. It wasn't
as long and it certainly wasn't fashionable, but it had a flavor
uniquely its own and was quite unlike any other street in the
world. It was "Main Street" for thousands of the newly arrived. And they brought to the street in microcosm what
their children would bring to the country at large. It was as
though a segment of the Old World had been up-rooted and
replanted along a single mile. Here were the Irish, gay and
quick-laughing and loving the hungry land they had left.
Germans came, hard-working and hard-drinking. The ghettos
of central Europe sent their contingent—tradesmen and in-
tellectuals and dreamers wise with sorrow. Men came from

Spain and Greece and Scotland and the plains of Africa. All met here and mingled and fought poverty and each other and married and did business and filled the air with Babel. And it was something to see. Lincoln would come and look and Charles Dickens, who was appalled by what he saw. The Bowery was not impressed by either. William Makepeace Thackeray, immaculate and Victorian, passed that way in search of copy. The story still lingers that he approached an idler on the outskirts of the neighborhood and announced that he wanted to visit the Bowery. The young Bowery Boy did not deign to raise his eyes. "Well, Sonny," he said, "you can go . . . as long as you don't stay too long."

Saturday night was the big night on the Bowery and a Saturday night in 1856 was the Bowery at its height. Stores stayed open long past midnight. Taverns flaunted their trade with huge transparencies enticing the unwary to delights within. Street hawkers conducted their business at the top of their lungs, selling clothing or food or jewelry that might have been stolen and was authentic or contrived and worthless. Some street vendors could outfit a man from hat to shoes out of their portable cases obligingly opened on the curb. There were "hot corn" girls and grimy newsboys and bootblacks grimier still. A tall man in a black, ill-fitting suit goes by carrying a sign: REPENT, REPENT, THE DAY OF THE LORD IS NEAR. Sailors, weary of the sea, swagger the streets with their shrill women and jostle newly arrived, gawking immigrants, and all are fair game for the hucksters and pickpockets and keepers of taverns. And over all hangs the acrid smell of smoke from the stands of food vendors and, in winter, from chimneys out of number.

There were an estimated five to ten thousand homeless children in New York and their begging and gamin enterprises gave some sections of the city an almost oriental aspect. Churchmen were beginning to recognize that there was a need for missions at their own doorstep, and many sermons were preached about it. From the distance of over a hundred years it would seem that there was a certain austerity in their concern for the homeless and ill-begotten. It was almost as if they believed that the children were, in some unfathomable way, guilty and their poverty a form of punishment. It was an unspoken response usually. But it was there. At a charity dinner in the Five Points one Thanksgiving, the children sang a song that had been composed especially for the occasion. One verse was revealing:

> "The dawn of hope is breaking,
> All doubt now disappears.
> The Five Points are awaking
> To penitential tears."

Penitential tears! Were there slums in the Sixth Ward? Were there hungry children there and depravity? Then someone had sinned. It was the curious anomaly of the nineteenth century that most people were never quite clear whose sin it was. Centuries earlier, Cotton Mather had taken sin away from John Milton and put it in the kitchen. Now Queen Victoria had made it unfashionable. By 1856 New Yorkers had added another indictment. Sin was also shabbily dressed. It explains a lot of what came later. A man with a diamond stickpin was not necessarily a saint but obviously the Lord looked kindly upon his affairs. Drunkenness was wrong. So was sloth. They both resulted in poverty. Virtue wore a top hat and carried a gold-handled cane.

This is one of the reasons why her generation hated Madame Restell, the dark-haired, black-eyed proprietress of a discreet establishment at 146 Greenwich Street. She was very evil. She was also very rich. It was a kind of treason.

Madame Restell was an abortionist. That's not her word.

In the advertisements she placed in the *Herald* and other
newspapers she referred to herself as a "professor of mid-
wifery" or "female physician." The wording of her advertisements was guarded but it was clear enough:

"To married women: Madame Restell is happy to have it
in her power to say that since the introduction into this
country about a year ago of her celebrated powders for maiden
ladies, hundreds have availed themselves of their use with
a success and satisfaction that has, at once, dispelled the fears
and doubts of the most timid and skeptical; for, notwith-
standing that for twenty years they have been used in Europe
with invariable success still some were inclined to entertain
some degree of distrust until become convinced of their successful adoption in this country."

She started out on Greenwich Street, moved to better
quarters at 160 Chambers Street and eventually built a huge
mansion on Fifth Avenue and Fifty-second Street across from
St. Patrick's Cathedral. That was a special victory for her.
She hated churchmen of any kind and, in buying the land,
had out-bid the diocese. And there she lived in squalid splen-
dor, practising her trade with profit and, in later years,
driving her carriage up to the Park. Children would run
alongside the carriage shouting, "Madame Killer!"—the
coachman would flick his whip on the horses' flanks and they
would break into a trot—"your house is built on babies'
skulls!"

Not by a flicker of the eye did she indicate that she heard.
But she heard.

Madame Restell had to be destroyed. She was a grotesque
and made all wealth seem evil. That big party she gave on
moving to Fifth Avenue. Disgraceful! People dancing downstairs and others maybe dying upstairs.

And there was another aspect to all this. The possibility
of pregnancy was a splendid deterrent to promiscuity in

women. Remove the threat and—well, women would be as free as men. A district attorney, arguing for a grand jury indictment of Madame Restell, made it quite clear where his fears lay:

"Certain acts have certain consequences? Not at all. All this is at an end. Madame Restell shows your spouse how she may commit as many adulteries as there are hours in the year without the possibility of detection."

The jurymen were impressed. Women should have rights but this was too much! The district attorney had made a point. And he warmed to the argument:

"Young man, you take to your bosom the image of purity, a thing upon which you think the stamp of God has been printed. That virgin bosom, that rosy cheek, that sparkling eye, assure you that the treasure is yours alone. Not so! Madame Restell's Preventative Powders have counterfeited the handwriting of nature. You have not a medal, fresh from the mint, but a base, lacquered counter that has undergone the sweaty contamination of a hundred palms."

It was too much, and the gentlemen voted to indict Madame Restell. Eventually she went to jail. But the advertising helped her business. And when she was destroyed, it was at a time of her own choosing and by her own hand and for her own reasons. She was facing trial again. She had, of course, evaded the law before. But she could never evade those children on the sidewalk. "Madame Killer!" She had an adopted daughter of her own whom she adored. And she had tried to hide from her the particulars of her craft. "Your house is built on babies' skulls," the children would shout.

One night Madame Restell stepped into the huge, ornate bathtub upstairs, eased her body into the warm, caressing water and slit her throat.

There were other activities in their fair city that the jurymen might have looked into. Gambling was open and easy to find. And houses of prostitution advertised through the mail. "Panel" houses were common in some sections of the city and for years proved highly profitable for the owners. This was a variation of the jealous husband game. A woman would make a contact on the street or in a saloon and take her victim to a room. The gas was turned low and her victim could see only that the walls were paneled. He would not guess that one of the panels was devised to slide back, giving access to the next room. A confederate was stationed there and while the victim was being beguiled by his new friend, her co-worker would slip into the room, snatch the man's purse, return and close the panel. Then would come an imperious knocking at the door and a demand to "Open up, by God. There's a man in there with you!" Invariably the victim would jump into his clothes and exit by a rear door or window. And he would be blocks away before checking his money. There was very little he could do. The police were silent partners in the business and a threat of publicity usually ended demands for prosecution.

Harriet Beecher Stowe's second novel about slavery, *Dred, a Tale of the Dismal Swamp,* was dramatized that year at the National Theater on Chatham Street. It was successful and, a week later, another version opened at the Bowery Theater. Phineas T. Barnum, never retiring where profits were concerned, produced his own version of the story, re-writing it and somehow introducing a midget into the narrative although no such character appeared in the book. This took a bit of ingenuity, but it provided a role for General Tom Thumb who was two feet, eleven inches high, appealing and under contract to Barnum.

Most theaters were located far downtown and in unfashionable areas. People of quality looked down on the theater and referred to it as an instrument of the devil. Only working people and the most daring social liberals went at all. One guide book of the period lists the theaters and describes them in some detail, but the author assured the reader that his information is all hearsay as he has never been in a theater in his life. However, there are some saloons described with such thinly veiled enthusiasm that the reader gets a mental picture of the author, foot on rail, telling the bartender how he is going to make a fortune writing guide books.

Resentment against the theater had been eased somewhat three years before with the tremendously successful production of *Uncle Tom's Cabin*. It told a fine moral story and made New Yorkers feel superior about the South. Hundreds of people who had never seen a play came to see this one. They enjoyed it enormously, talked about it all their lives, and never went again. Even Henry Ward Beecher, the very prominent pastor of the huge Plymouth Church in Brooklyn, crossed over on the ferry to the Bowery to see how his sister's book looked as a play. A. H. Purdy, manager of the theater, was so impressed by the visit of the Reverend Mr. Beecher that he determined that the incident would be forever recorded. Purdy posed for an oil painting of himself holding the Bible in one hand and a copy of *Uncle Tom's Cabin* in the other. The painting was hung in the theater lobby along with various quotations from the Bible.

New York was big, crowded, rough, harsh, loud, law-breaking and in a hurry. Some of its citizens were getting rich, and it was an unprecedented wealth, unlike the land-oriented wealth of earlier times. Daniel Drew, shrewd and conspiring and Bible-quoting and illiterate, had made his first million and was elected a director of the Erie Railroad. "I got to be a millionaire before I know'd it, hardly," was how he explained it to a reporter.

Cornelius Vanderbilt was worth much more and had begun his assault on New York society. They respected his millions but deplored his vocabulary which was brightly spiced with anatomical allusions learned from the wharfs where he had started out. Jay Gould, predatory, avaricious and saying little, had arrived in New York and was looking for a promising business for an enterprising young man.

Jim Fisk was still a New England peddler, but was restive. All would win in the struggle for wealth. All were alike in a belief that moral rules were an imposition and an invention useful only to those who knew no other way to fight.

Many people thought that way. And what was sin on the Bowery or the Five Points was cleverness on Wall Street and a thing to be admired. It was the essence of the double standard. And it expressed itself in many ways. A politician who did not wear a diamond stick pin was inadequate and not to be trusted. He simply had not taken advantage of the opportunities presented to him. Women could sin and, when they did, were referred to as "fallen sisters" and were more to be pitied than censured. Poor people could sin and, if not watched carefully, probably would. And respectability was not earned so much as it was bought. It was bought by contributions to charity.

Drew was a perfect example. As a young man he used to drive cattle down the Hudson and Mohawk Valleys to the markets of New York. The beauty of the legend-haunted hills and dawn over the river so fired his young mind that he was inspired to new heights, and he conceived a most ingenious plan. He devised a route that, in its final stretches, bypassed all streams or ponds so that, a day or so before arrival, his herd was practically mad with thirst. As added security, he fed the animals salt. Then, just before they were to be weighed by the purchasers, he turned them loose in a nearby stream where in a short time they drank enough water to make him a rich man.

In later enterprises the technique changed but the basic theme was the same . . . to sell what one owned at a price

higher than its intrinsic value. Then one might give money
to build a church. Drew built two. He also donated a quarter
of a million dollars to found the Drew Theological Seminary
at Madison, New Jersey. Incidentally, he articulated for
future generations the basic error to be avoided in the technique of selling short: "He who sells what isn't his'n must
buy it back or go to prison."

The mayor of New York in 1857 was almost a distillation
of all the weaknesses and strengths of the time and place. His
name was Fernando Wood. He was unscrupulous, imagina-
tive, ambitious and exquisitely deceptive, and he served as
a teacher and master craftsman to those who, even then,
were watching him with envy and admiration.

Despite his mildly exotic given name, Fernando came from
stern middle-class Quaker stock. His father was a cigar maker
from Philadelphia who moved to New York shortly after
Fernando was born. The name was his mother's idea. Before
his birth, she had been reading a novel called *The Three
Spaniards,* and the name "Fernando" seemed to embody all
that was dashing and admirable. By the time he was twenty,
Fernando had a cigar shop of his own which he gave up to
run a groggery on Rector Street. Later, when he entered
politics, this was euphemistically referred to as a "grocery
store." It was only a half lie, which shows that Fernando
wasn't really trying. You could buy some vegetables there if
you wished. But you could also get flowers on the Bowery
and that didn't make that the gardens of Fontainebleau.

Wood made enough money selling rum to buy three sailing ships which he engaged in coastwise trade. This proved
highly profitable and he was able to add five more to his fleet.

But Wood wanted more out of life than just money. In
1840, when he was twenty-eight, he ran for Congress and was
elected. He had one last fling with business when gold was
discovered in California. He sent a supply ship to the west

coast and by cheating his partner out of his share of the profits made enough money to retire. He would later tell biographers that he spent the next few years trying to repair an "imperfect early education." It was modest of him to say that. For the career he planned, the years he spent running that grog shop were better than the education of Henry Adams.

Wood turned naturally to Tammany. In earlier years he had been a Know-Nothing, a sometime-secret group who, when asked about the organization, responded that they knew nothing about it. But it was well organized even down to password phrases, one of which was, "Have you seen Sam?" George Washington was their patron saint, the "Star-Spangled Banner" their emblem, and anti-foreignism their way of life. They were, in short, anti-immigrant, anti-Irish, anti-Catholic, anti-German, anti-anything that was not "native American." Tammany itself had reflected this feeling in earlier years but the battles with the Whigs had drawn that organization closer and closer to the newly arrived, and by 1857 the name Tammany was almost synonymous with immigrant.

Wood's enemies tried to destroy him as a vote-getter by bringing up his Know-Nothing past. But they were dealing with a master in the techniques of propaganda. He organized whispering squads who in "native" American neighborhoods boasted of Wood's anti-foreign feelings. Other hired hands along the Bowery and the Five Points were denying the whole thing and painting him as the immigrant's only true friend among the councils of the great. Some of his earlier business transactions were published in the newspapers. Wood was unconcerned. "The people," he said, "will elect me mayor though I should commit a murder in my family between now and the election."

He was right. Despite a largely hostile press, despite the

fact that most of the influential people in the city were against him Wood was elected mayor.

The Sixth Ward that year cast four hundred more votes than there were voters.

The enthusiasm for reform which had pitched the Forty Thieves out of City Hall had largely dissipated. But there was one final move. In 1857, the financial affairs of the city were taken out of the hands of the aldermen and vested in a twelve-man Board of Supervisors. It was a splendid idea. The law specified that there were to be six from the Whig or—as they were now—the Republican Party, and six from the Democratic Party. They would be elected by popular vote and hence free from the pressures of special groups. The Republicans would watch the Democrats and the Democrats would watch the Republicans. And no one would have free access to the city's coffers. It was perfect . . .

Almost. William Marcy Tweed, ex-congressman and ex-alderman, was elected a supervisor.

Tweed was delighted. This was better than being in Congress. It was even better than being an alderman. The supervisors were in charge of public improvements, taxations and all areas involving income and expenditure. Such matters are always complicated and, to the unimaginative, uninteresting. He would not be bothered now by nosy newspaper reporters. It was basically a bookkeeping job. And, properly done, there need never be an audit of the books. Kansas-Nebraska Bill indeed!

One of the duties of the supervisors was to appoint the inspectors of elections. These were important men in the functioning of the city government. They stayed at the polls on election days and made certain that there were no illegal voters. Six against six. The Republicans would not permit the selection of an inspector who would overlook ballot stuffing by Tammany "repeaters." And the Democrats were equally alert to any such attempts on the part of the Republicans. Maybe there would be honest inspectors for a change. And honest elections where you would really know who got the most votes.

There weren't. On the day the selection of inspectors was to be made, one of the Republican members did not appear. It was now six against five, and Tweed and the other Democrats were able to pick whom they wished. Years later, the reason for the absence that day of the Republican member was made clear. He had been given $2,500 to stay away.

It was very easy. And from that moment on Tweed controlled the Board. In a sense, he was the Board.

Experiments in graft began on a fairly diminished basis. The word went out that all bills rendered the city were to be padded. The contractor, whether he was selling services or goods, would figure out his true bill and add fifteen percent. He would be paid and immediately kick back the extra fifteen percent in cash. Later the padding was raised to twenty-five percent. It would go to fifty-five—sixty-five . . .

Tweed hired some underlings to help and bolstered his position with a few jobs on the side. He became a "sachem" of Tammany Hall and later Grand Sachem. He was also Deputy Street Commissioner. That sounds like a modest job and it was. But it paid money. This was the only question Tweed asked. And he reached out for more.

There wasn't much more. Not yet. Because of that damned Mayor Wood.

Tweed watched. Sooner or later everyone makes a mistake. So will Wood. He's no saint. He just acts like one.

Watch his mistakes. Everybody makes them. Just watch. And, when the time comes, act.

Mayor Wood was no saint, true. But he was smart. After he was elected in 1854, he surprised everybody by conducting himself as a very model mayor. He passed a proclamation closing saloons on Sundays and, within two weeks, there were only about twenty that stayed open on that day. There are no figures on the subject but one imagines they must have been terribly crowded. Previously some twenty-three hundred had stayed open. There was a good deal of head-shaking down at Tammany Hall, an ornate, four-story building at Frankfort and Nassau Streets. Wood was acting like a damned reform mayor. Some old-line Tammanyites publicly praised him but privately expressed the hope that he would drown in a barrel of non-alcoholic sarsaparilla. Was he out of his mind? Later, when Wood piously returned a season pass that had been sent to him by an omnibus company, they were sure of it.

But this was just the beginning. The Mayor arranged to have the streets cleaned better than they ever had been before; he closed a number of brothels and gambling houses; waged a severe campaign against pickpockets; and even saw to it that cartmen did not overcharge for their services. There was a complaint book set up in City Hall and all citizens were invited to register their private thoughts on how the city should be run. No one dreamed that Mr. Wood had the most private thoughts of all on the subject.

He was modestly deprecating when temperance groups began speaking of him as the next governor, and was probably amused when a delegation of voters came all the way from Iowa to urge him to run for President of the United States.

He had other plans. In 1856 he ran again for Mayor. And this time he showed his true colors. The police patrolled the voting places and frequently kept anti-Wood people from voting. There were riots, broken heads and broken ballot boxes. The saloon keepers, the basic unit now of city politics, were wooed back by a promise that, if elected, the Mayor would allow them to practice their craft on Sundays.

He was re-elected. Opponents said that ten thousand fraudulent votes had been cast for Wood. But he won. And the fun would begin . . .

Wood immediately began selling public offices with the understanding that the officeholder would get his money back as best he could at the expense of the city. He let the street-cleaning contract for $279,000 although a responsible contractor had offered to do the same work for $195,000. In addition, the successful bidder had to pay an additional $40,000 tab to get the measure through the Common Council and there was a yearly gratuity to the Wood family of $69,750.

Conservatives were appalled and angered. Saloons were opened again on Sundays, and the talk about Wood for Governor stopped. And no more visitors came east from Iowa.

Wood was unconcerned. He was deep in the trough and no one could stop him now.

But they could try. Conservative elements took their case to the state legislature. This body pondered things for awhile and came up with a rather astonishing measure. They abolished the New York City Police Department—the "Municipals" they were called—and established a state police in New York City called the Metropolitan Police Force. Appointment power in the Street Cleaning Department was also taken away from Wood and vested in the Governor. Let the Mayor ponder that for awhile.

Wood didn't ponder long. He called both laws illegal and refused to recognize them. He knew that most of the policemen were Democrats and would support him in the emergency. And he was right. A poll was taken, and eight hundred of the eleven hundred city policemen voted to abide with His Honor, the Mayor. The three hundred Republican policemen were fired from the force and were promptly hired by the state authorities as the nucleus of the new metropolitan force. When eight hundred more were added to the

"Metropolitans," Wood responded by appointing another three hundred to the municipal force, and New York found itself with two police forces of equal size neither of which recognized the authority of the other.

For awhile both forces patrolled the streets; in some neighborhoods the police seemed to outnumber the citizens. The situation was inherently unstable and was bound to result in trouble. Questions of authority between the two forces, at first discussed soberly and impersonally, soon degenerated into speculations as to whose parents weren't married, and the battles began. It was a little like the gang wars that New Yorkers were familiar with, except that there was discipline now and the contestants were being paid for the entertainment. The rowdies of the Bowery and Five Points enjoyed the spectacle enormously and frequently acted as agents provocateur when things threatened to get dull. Sentimentally they were with Wood's "municipals," of course, but with splendid sportsmanship they would gladly advise members of the metropolitan force when one of their members was hardpressed or outnumbered. It wasn't whether they won or lost, but how they played the game. News of New York's peculiar troubles got around, and thugs, confidence men and pickpockets poured in from Newark, Boston and Philadelphia to practice their crafts and partake in the general carnival atmosphere.

But the whole thing was too good to last. The issue had to be resolved and, thanks to the somewhat less than model mayor, it had to end in violence and pain.

The showdown came on Tuesday, June 16, 1857. Several days earlier the Street Commissioner had died and the state authorities had decided to appoint one Daniel D. Conover to the job. He was a Republican, loyal to the Albany group, and he might even have known something about New York City streets. Mayor Wood refused to recognize the state's appointment and looked around for a candidate of his own. He settled upon a man named Charles Devlin who impressed Wood tremendously with his qualifications—i.e., $50,000 cash for the appointment.

Conover arrived at City Hall that Tuesday morning, walked briskly up the steps with some friends and announced that he was ready to start work. Mayor Wood ordered him to leave and, when Conover resorted to argument on the merits of the case, had him thrown out.

Conover went to a judge (Republican) and had a warrant sworn out for the Mayor's arrest.

This posed an interesting problem in municipal protocol. Who would arrest the Mayor? No one on the municipal force would dream of such a thing, warrant or not, and no one on the metropolitan force could really be said to relish the job. There just happened to be about nine hundred municipal policemen wandering around in City Hall and the Park outside. If anyone wants to put the Mayor in jail, just send him to us . . .

The job fell to a hard-jawed, veteran policeman named Captain George W. Walling, late of the municipal and now of the metropolitan police. Curiously enough, he was allowed to enter City Hall and walk into the Mayor's office. Wood was waiting. He didn't like Walling. Walling was tough. Well, he had dealt with tough characters before in that grog shop called grocery on Rector Street. Their conversation was restrained and formal. Wood spoke first:

"Well, Sir, what do you want of me?"

"I have a warrant here for your arrest."

"You are not an officer. I dismissed you from the force."

"I am an officer. I am a member of the metropolitan police."

"I do not recognize the legality of the service or the existence of the metropolitan police. I will not submit to arrest, or go with you, or concede that you are an officer."

"I shall have to take you forcibly if you resist."

"I will not be taken. You can consider that resistance if you please."

"No," said Walling and, for some reason, he was smiling, "No, Sir, that is not resistance . . . only refusal."

Walling started to move toward the Mayor. Wood pressed a button. Three doors opened into the Mayor's office and a half a dozen policemen crowded through each one. Walling was quickly pushed out into the corridor. Then he was escorted briskly to the street.

The municipal and metropolitan police had frequently battled it out on the streets. Now they would fight in City Hall itself. The news traveled up to the Bowery and within minutes the little park in front of City Hall was crowded with spectators. Not that anyone cared much who won. When two police forces battle, everybody wins. Bets were offered and covered on the outcome. A newspaper man observed that one spectator wore a hat band on which were written the words, "No King!" It still isn't entirely clear what he meant.

The "Metropolitans" arrived in due time. They were greeted with groans from the eager spectators. There were only fifty of them. They marched briskly up the front steps toward the waiting "Municipals."

It wasn't much of a battle, really. The Bowery Boys commented later that they had often put on much better shows. It was fifty men against more than eight hundred and it didn't last long. The "Metropolitans" were pushed back down the steps. Some spectators joined in the fun but they weren't needed. The "Metropolitans" were badly beaten. Twelve of them were seriously injured.

The day seemed to be about over. Some of the Bowery Boys started wandering back. But a few blocks uptown the Seventh Regiment, under the command of a general of the state militia, was marching down Broadway enroute to Boston to take part in a ceremony marking the anniversary of the Battle of Bunker Hill. Members of the state Board of Police Commissioners intercepted them and told them about the fight at City Hall. Moments later, the regiment marched into the area before City Hall and came to a military halt. Mayor Wood looked out of his window and all he could see was rifles. He could handle one metropolitan policeman in his office. He could handle fifty policemen on the City Hall steps. But a whole regiment was too much. This wasn't just a municipal misunderstanding. This was war.

He submitted to arrest and was promptly released in $10,000 bail. It took long months of court litigation to settle the question of police authority and Wood finally lost. The municipal force was disbanded. Later Wood was a little disconcerted to learn that when the Seventh Regiment marched into City Hall Park they were not carrying ammunition.

Tweed admired the Mayor's courage. He liked his audacity. But Wood had lost. Tweed noted that in particular. It was almost time to take him on. Meanwhile, for anyone interested in the dynamics of civic maladministration, Wood was a splendid teacher.

One lesson that he taught was that you could defy reformers and advocates of honest, representative government if you had numbers on your side. The vote of a butcher's apprentice counts equally with that of a millionaire. And it's a lot easier to get. Let them have their peasant pleasures. Pretend you have their interests in mind and they will be your slaves. Above all do not interfere in their games. A riot is an indication of unease and discontent. No one riots after a heavy meal. And if the Five Pointers and Bowery gangsters were rich, they wouldn't be for you. Hunger—other people's hunger, at least—has its uses.

It was a terribly dangerous game. But Wood played it

superbly. Inherent in any despotism, of course, is the question as to who are the slaves and who the master. Perhaps Wood knew that. He would leave it for others to resolve. Already there were hints . . .

The Fourth of July came that year in the midst of the confusion over the two police departments. In the nineteenth century, Americans took this holiday rather more seriously than now. Many of our holidays are borrowed. But this one is uniquely ours. And Americans a century ago always made the most of it. It was a more important day than Christmas which, until discovered by Mr. Dickens, was one of the lesser of the year's special days.

In 1857, July Fourth fell on a Saturday. And it began early. By dawn, units of the First, Second, Third and Fourth Brigades of the New York State Militia were forming in Fourteenth Street, and by seven-thirty, they stretched from river to river. Governor King reviewed them at Union Square. Then they paraded down Broadway to City Hall Park for another review by the Mayor.

The Park was jammed. The forecast had been for rain, but it was a delightful day and it seemed that all New York had converged down on the one-time "common" before City Hall. A reporter for the *Herald* left a picture of what it was like to be at that place on that day. Stalls had been set up and everything was for sale—iced lemonade, ice cream, gingerbread, nuts, oranges, cakes, sarsaparilla—and there were fast-talking gentlemen who offered fantastic bargains to the uncritical and trusting:

"Here you are, Sir. Only six cents. First you have a fine collection of songs, next some practical advice, then a fifty dollar bill, and with this I put in a plain gold ring, a chased gold ring, a fine enameled ring, each of them a fine present for your lady love, worth twice the money asked for the whole. Then I give you a beautiful gold scarf pin, a lady's silver thimble, a fine comb and a new penny inside of which you will find six of the smallest silver spoons you ever saw. And all for six cents! There's a few more left. If you want them, now's the time. You take one? Ah, thank you, Sir . . ."

His stall was opposite that of a man who offered a peek into a "Cosmorama," a device for magnifying pictures and giving them a three dimensional effect:

"Only one cent to see the greatest picture of the age. Here you have the picture of the Vatican at Rome. Next you have the Pope with his toenails pared and cleaned exactly as they was before they was kissed by ex-President Fillmore. Next you have the Bridge of Sighs, so-called from the fact that so many disappointed young ladies having thrown themselves into the river, which is not visible on account of the size of the machine . . ."

The troops came and were reviewed and left with the cheering ringing in their ears. Everyone stayed around because there were to be fireworks at nightfall from the roof of City Hall. There were musicians who played for pennies and children who danced and passed the hat. Late in the afternoon, a boy who had climbed one of the trees in the park developed a "rip in his unmentionables, which, giving undue prominence to his posterior development, raised a prolonged shout of laughter. Trying to regain his former position in order to screen himself from further merriment, the boy had just taken hold of the nearest branch when it gave way and down he came souse in a bucket of soda water syrup."

Vagrant music and the hope of fireworks to come. It was pretty tame entertainment.

In the mid-afternoon some young men, residents of the Sixth Ward just to the north, started wandering back home. On the Bowery things were at least that exciting every day.

And with a little imagination and nerve you could have some real fun . . .

It's hard to tell just how it began. In the pre-dawn of that day some Dead Rabbits and a few mobsters from other Five Point gangs had invaded the Bowery chanting "Down with the Bowery Boys." It was not an action calculated to keep matters serene. But, incredibly, it seems to have passed unchallenged. Perhaps most of the enemy were asleep. The Five Pointers continued their violation of territory and, turning a corner, spotted a member of the hated metropolitan police. Their cry changed to "Down with the metropolitan police" and "Down with black Republicans." The policeman took refuge in an all-night coffee shop. Normally the Bowery patrons would have resented the intrusion of a policeman there but when they saw his dilemma they gave him refuge. It didn't last long. The Five Pointers rushed the place, beat it open and found to their chagrin that the policeman and his new-found friends had slipped out the back door. Another policeman who sought safety in a saloon took advantage of the same escape route. And reluctantly but triumphantly, the Five Pointers drifted back to the Sixth Ward and to a sleep that comes only to those who have labored long and well.

Shopkeepers and the un-violent on the Bowery hoped that, the next day being a holiday, the incident might go unavenged. They were wrong. The Bowery Boys spent the day gathering their forces. By late afternoon they were ready. There were three hundred of them. This wouldn't be just another fight. This would be a real battle.

They went about their tasks with devotion and dedication. Carts and wagons parked at the curbs were expertly unlocked and dragged along. And from somewhere a number of mattresses were requisitioned. Members of Wood's municipal force joined the growing army. They carried clubs and pistols. Women marched along with them, and children. One boy had a pickax. No one questioned this as a cumbersome weapon. It was to dig up paving blocks. Slowly and somberly they marched that hot Fourth of July afternoon to the street where their Seventh Ward bordered on the hated Sixth. Here, and it's reminiscent of the street fighting in Paris, they set up barricades. The carts were overturned and the mattresses tied down.

News of this defiant act came, of course, to the Five Pointers. Within minutes almost, they had formed their army. It was of about equal size. And they, too, set up barricades. A mile or so downtown people were having fun. *Iced lemonade —ice cream—then I give you a beautiful gold scarf pin . . .* And on the border of the Bowery and the Five Points, men were preparing for a fight. They were willing to kill and to take the chance of being killed, and some of them would do both. And it was never entirely clear to anyone what it was all about.

For awhile they were satisfied simply to crouch behind their barricades and shoot at each other. Then about fifty of the Bowery Boys charged the enemy defenses. They scrambled over their own barricades and moved with almost military precision down the street.

The attack was beaten off. From the surrounding houses came a shower of missiles—bottles, flat-irons, candlesticks— and they were forced back. The boy with the pickax was killed. He had been shot through the heart. The firing blended with the sound of fireworks from all over the city and there were people a short two blocks away who did not know that anything unusual was going on. A fourteen-year-old boy, a bystander who lived with his mother at 119 Mulberry Street, was struck by an errant bullet. It entered his head under the right eye and lodged under his tongue. Incredibly he lived long enough to run back to the Bowery shouting, "Where is the doctor?" He died in a drug store.

The battle raged an hour before news of it came to the police. They were ill-prepared. Most of the officials had taken the day off and others had been dispatched to various ceremonies around town. It was a group of only twenty-five who marched down to Mulberry Street to end this disturbance of the holiday peace.

But it was a lot more than a simple disturbance of the peace. The police flanked the Dead Rabbits' barricade and came up from the rear. The Five Pointers opened fire on this new attack. One policeman fell dead and several others were wounded. They stayed long enough to return the fire and then they fled. The Dead Rabbits counter-charged and managed to catch up with some of the policemen who were less fleet than their fellows. When they returned to the barricades, some of the Dead Rabbits were wearing policemen's badges.

For hours the battle raged back and forth, with neither side a clear winner. Toward nightfall a curious incident occurred. A metropolitan policeman approached the barricade of the Bowery Boys. He was alone, armed with a club. Instantly he was covered from a dozen angles. "Don't shoot," he said. "I come as a friend. I want to lead you." Incredibly they accepted him and he did lead them. He had been a friend of a policeman killed by the Dead Rabbits. And the fight for him was a personal one.

He led well. Waving his club, he charged the Five Pointers' barricade with the Bowery Boys close behind. And they succeeded in driving the Dead Rabbits back. Again there was a counter-charge and a stalemate.

News of the rioting spread throughout the city. The police commissioner finally swallowed his pride, searched out Isaiah Rynders and asked him to stop the fighting. Exultant and triumphant, Rynders made his way down to the Bowery and appeared before the barricades. He raised his arms and announced that it was time for everyone to go home. Enough blood had been shed and . . .

A shower of bricks slammed down around him and he had to flee. Rynders, friend of the unwashed and unwanted, and he, too, is expelled from this place! It was a warning. Or it should have been. Who the master here and who the slave?

The rumor started that the mobs planned to attack the fashionable areas of the city. Children were called home, doors and windows locked, and homeowners hastily loaded up guns that had not been fired for years and took their stand at the door step.

It didn't happen. Not yet. The riot rumbled to a slow, reluctant and, of course, inconclusive end. All this was just rehearsal. It had not been planned. It had simply happened. Given enough people living in the starkest of poverty and add heat and boredom and sullen resentment, and the result is forewritten. Slaves do not choose their slavery. And they do not love their masters. They didn't love Rynders. They didn't love Wood.

Heat and propinquity and never quite enough to eat. Add leadership to this and a purpose, combine the gangs and take into their ranks all the other angry, hungry people, and they can take over a city. They can take over any city. And they would take this one.

It began Monday morning, July 13, 1863. There was smoke over the lower city. It came from fires deliberately set. The smoke lay motionless and ominous like a gathering cloud. Then, faintly, you could hear their voices. It was the gangs again.

And this time they weren't fighting each other. They were marching side by side. And they were coming uptown . . .

CHAPTER 5

THERE WAS A CROOKED MAN

> "There was a crooked man, and he
> Went a crooked mile,
> And he found a crooked sixpence
> Against a crooked stile;
> He bought a crooked cat which
> Caught a crooked mouse,
> And they all lived together in
> a little crooked house."
> — *Mother Goose.*

THERE IS STILL STANDING in the city of New York a low, squat, time-haunted building, toad-like and incredibly ugly, that could well serve as the epitaph for William Marcy Tweed. He built it and he made it the way it is. And in a curious way it looks like him. It is ponderous and heavy and it seems to seek the shadows rather than the sun. It stands just behind the lovely City Hall building and is hidden from the park and the City Hall steps where traditionally distinguished visitors are made welcome. None of these ever sees the old buildings in the back. Like a member of the family who is kept upstairs when visitors arrive, it's not quite presentable.

In 1858, when Tweed was a member of the Board of Supervisors, it was proposed that a county courthouse be

101

built. All were in agreement, and an expenditure of $250,000 was allowed. There were delays, however, and work was not begun until 1862. The $250,000 was soon exhausted and Tweed and his fellow members obtained authorization to raise another $800,000 to complete the building. Tweed quickly indicated, however, that this sum was not sufficient and the legislature authorized the expenditure of another $600,000. It was 1865 now and the building was coming along nicely. But the next year another $600,000 was requested and duly appropriated. The building was almost finished now. Another $750,000, they said, should take care of everything.

Of course, there were repairs that had to be made—a few hundred thousand was needed for that. And the building had to be furnished and stocked with supplies. There had to be carpets, for example, shades and curtains. The cost of these was figured at $675,534.41.

What was happening was simple and stark. With no one having access to the records of the Board of Supervisors, they were free to pay any amount they wished for goods and services. All persons doing business with the city were instructed to pad the bills submitted to the city. The face value of the bill would be paid and then the contractor would reimburse the city auditor the amount—or nearly the amount—of the excess payment. A plasterer named Andrew J. Garvey achieved a fragile immortality by earning $133,187.20 for two days' repair work. In two years, his income from the city, on the books at least, was over two million dollars. Mr. Garvey very graciously used to decorate Tammany Hall free of charge every Fourth of July.

Tweed must have waited for a reaction to the enormous expense of the new courthouse. There was none. No one knew. The ledgers were kept private. Well, let's see, gentlemen. Shall we proceed further? The judges will need safes, for example.

A man named J. McBride Davidson, owner of a safe supply office in Duane Street, got the contract. He charged the city $404,347.72. Mr. Davidson had a little private bar in the rear of his office where Tweed and his associates were treated to fine wines while matters of business were discussed.

And they could even afford to be careless. Seventy-five hundred dollars for thermometers. Awnings for the new courthouse were bought for $41,746.83. There were $2,676.75 worth of locks on the judges' chambers, and "brooms, etc." cost another $41,190.95.

Tweed was getting rich. He was, of course, at the mercy of the city auditor. But he handled this situation neatly. He gave the job to a quietly efficient man named James Watson who had compelling reasons of his own to honor secrets and to be discreet.

In 1850, Watson was the proprietor of a small business in New York, plagued by competition and rising costs and totally unaware that he was marked for greatness. His business failed and when creditors became insistent, Watson fled to California. He was brought back under arrest and placed in Ludlow Street Jail. Here he came to the attention of the warden who apparently admired his handwriting. Unfortunately, no sample of Watson's handwriting seems to have survived, but it must have been exceedingly good. At any event, by the time of his discharge he was handling all the official accounts of the Ludlow Street Jail.

The warden brought his former charge to the attention of the Sheriff and Watson became collector for the Sheriff's office. He served under three sheriffs and then became city auditor. Tweed kept him in the job. He was a man who could be trusted to be discreet. No one had to approach a supervisor with any proposals. You talked to Jimmy. It saved embarrassment on both sides. Watson lived in glory in a home at Forty-second Street and Madison Avenue. His salary was $1,500 a year. But he was, he told everyone, very fortunate in his Wall Street investments.

No one ever saw his books. And no one ever would have seen them had not Jimmy had a predilection for fast horses. But that came later.

Slowly the county courthouse took shape. And it's still there—that building, squat and ugly and a monument to greed. Its final cost can never be precisely determined because some of the expenses were charged to other county buildings. But it was certainly not less than $13,000,000. This is about four times the cost of the Houses of Parliament.

Tweed moved uptown.

He was getting rich. And people deferred to him. His affairs were not mentioned frequently in the papers but somehow his name was always being spoken. No one quite knew why. But the twisted web of New York politics in the early 1860's seemed always to lead back to William Marcy Tweed and the little office that he rented at 95 Duane Street. WILLIAM MARCY TWEED, it said on the door, ATTORNEY AT LAW.

Tweed had many visitors there. And some he would take with him into history. There was Peter B. Sweeny. Tweed had helped him in his campaign to become district attorney back in 1857. Sweeny was short—"stunted," one observer called him—with "sinister" features. He had a low forehead, coarse, black hair and mustache, deep, penetrating eyes and an appetite for money almost as great as Tweed's. He thought of himself as looking like Napoleon, the Third, and admitted that he admired him. Sweeny would become one of the "Ring" which was now in the process of being formed. And he would be a worthy member, giving services rendered for compensation received. He was a man of vigor but also of sullen quietness. And he was constantly plotting. Indeed, his whole life seems to be one giant conspiracy.

Sweeny was born on Park Row in New York City about 1824. His mother ran a liquor store and used to wait on customers while nursing young Peter. As a young man he worked for awhile as a waiter in the saloon his father was running in Jersey City. He seemed to have known that this arena was not worthy of his talents and he struck out. He went to St. Peter's Parochial School in Barclay Street, New York, where his marks were at least good enough to get him into Columbia College. Later he studied law, spent some time as a lobbyist in Albany where his uncle, Thomas J. Barr, was a state senator.

When he was elected district attorney, it looked as if his career was fairly started. But at his first trial, he lost his self-possession completely and resigned in humiliation.

He might have left politics except for the influence of a shrewd, clever bookkeeper known as "Slippery Dick." His real name was Richard B. Connolly. He had been born in a small town near Cork, Ireland, where his father was a schoolmaster who enjoyed some local celebrity because he had married an heiress. Young Richard got a fairly good education in Ireland and then migrated to Philadelphia. There was a misunderstanding apparently with a person identified only as "a market woman" and Connolly found it expedient to remove to New York City. He got a job in the Custom House and, clever with figures, moved up to the position of discount clerk at the Bank of North America. His excellent record there, precision with figures and attention to detail, would recommend him highly to former Congressman Tweed. The fact that no one seemed to trust Connolly disturbed Tweed not at all. Connolly had imagination and nerve. What's integrity? Tweed could find that in any bank clerk.

In 1851, Connolly was the Tammany nominee for county clerk. He won and Tweed was impressed. Connolly was re-elected in 1854. And he didn't even need his own vote. An opponent who had discovered that Connolly had never bothered to become naturalized, waited at the polls all day for Connolly to show up so that he could face him with this interesting fact and maybe there could be a discussion about a candidate for county clerk who was not even a citizen.

Connolly stayed home and won the election. Tweed liked that. A man after his own heart. They began seeing more and more of each other. And the talks got longer and longer.

Connolly's family crest bore the motto: *En Dieu Est Tout.* It showed a mauled hand holding a ring.

Then there was Abraham Oakey Hall. "Elegant" Oakey Hall he was usually called. Mr. Hall had been a Republican, but he left the Republican ranks when they nominated Abraham Lincoln. He simply would not stay in a political party that nominated a boorish oaf for the presidency.

Hall was smart. He would in the years ahead play the role of a clown, wearing, on demand, ridiculous clothes and using the English language like a music hall comedian. He loved puns. Speaking once at a meeting called to consider Oriental immigration problems, he noted the warmth of the evening and remarked that it was appropriate in discussing "the coolie question." But he was clever enough. He was a writer of plays that were only half bad; he was quite conversant with the classics; and he was a more than brilliant lawyer. He was competent in many areas, but could never really decide what role to play. Once, after Tweed had made him mayor, he said that he would rather have been the editor of a paper like the *Herald* than President of the United States. He probably would have made a good editor. He was a dreadful mayor.

Hall was born in New York of a respectable family which claimed descent from one of Cromwell's colonels. He went to New York University and Harvard Law School. He tried his hand at writing for awhile and at newspaper reporting. He was appointed assistant district attorney and, after the death of the district attorney, took over the job. Later he was elected to that office. He came to Tweed's office at 95 Duane Street. He felt quite at home there. Tweed liked him. He liked his cheap jokes and over-elegant clothes. And he understood Hall. These jokes, these pompous allusions to the classics, they really hid a soaring ambition. But Hall didn't want money. He wanted recognition and fame and applause. Tweed could provide that in abundance. Someone to cheer and applaud and slap you on the back? Tweed had them by the thousands. Hall came and came again . . .

But Tweed was not yet fulfilled. He resented sharing his power with the other members of the Board of Supervisors. But most of all he hated Wood. Wood was not one of his boys. Wood had his own ideas and his own system of plunder and his own chain of command. From the beginning, Tweed had realized that Wood had to be destroyed. It was Tweed or Wood. One of them had to go. The city wasn't big enough for both. One of them would have to go.

It was Wood. And the fight was surprisingly easy. It wasn't that he was too corrupt. It was simply that he had become old-fashioned. Tweed was of the new school. His rascality was masked behind pious words about his services to the people. Wood was flagrant. He shocked people. He lacked finesse.

Like the time they had to sell City Hall at a public auction. Wood shouldn't have permitted that. It was bad public relations. He wasn't mayor at the time, but the beginnings went right back to him and everyone knew it.

It all came out when a Wall Street broker named Robert W. Lowber brought suit against the city for abrogation of contract. During Wood's administration, Lowber had made a rather profitable deal with the city. They promised to buy—

for $196,000—a piece of land in which he had equity. The land was worth perhaps $60,000. It was an obvious steal. Lowber only had $20,000 equity in the property. And the new Common Council quite properly refused to follow through on the contract.

Quite properly but, as the court pointed out, quite illegally. The sanctity of a contract is not easily violated. Lowber won $196,000 judgment. With interest, cost of the trial and damages, it came to $228,000. Tired of the delay, Lowber placed judgment for this sum in the hands of the sheriff.

Under the law, the sheriff had only one course of action. He had to find city property equal to the amount demanded and sell it at public auction.

City Hall struck him as a nice building. It was a little old, perhaps, but it wore well. One wonders what old Edward Livingston would have thought had he known on that day back in 1803 that the building would one day be knocked down to the highest bidder to pay for a false debt. Livingston knew about debts and the payment thereof.

A notice was duly posted announcing the sale of City Hall. The city's new mayor, Daniel F. Tiemann, a reform mayor, was devastated at the news. There was a rumor that Wood planned to bid for the building, turn it into a headquarters for his followers and, as an insulting gesture, announce that city employees could continue to use the building at his pleasure.

Tiemann decided to bid for the building himself. As it turned out, Wood did not appear. Neither did any other would-be buyers and Tiemann had the sale all to himself. He became the owner briefly until the city bought it back from him at the sale price.

That price, incidentally, was $50,000.

Then there was the time that Wood, back now in the

mayor's chair, sent a message to the Common Council suggesting that New York City secede from the Union. It was January 7, 1861. Lincoln had been elected but had not yet taken office. Two days before, the *Star of the West* had sailed from New York with men and arms for the relief of Fort Sumter. The sailing was supposed to be secret, but a southern sympathizer had become privy to the plan and had telegraphed the news to the South. The *Star of the West* was fired on and turned back. South Carolina had seceded and others would follow. New York City was strongly southern in sympathy. Lincoln was, after all, a Republican. Wood himself had close connections with the South. He and his brother, Benjamin Wood, owned lotteries that had been chartered by southern states.

If South Carolina could secede . . . Wood pondered long and hard.

Imagine New York City as an independent city-state! It could be one giant customs house. The trade of all Europe would filter through. It would be perhaps the smallest, but— by God!—the richest nation in the world! And he would be mayor. President maybe?

A message from the Mayor for the consideration of the Common Council:

"It would seem that a dissolution of the Federal Union is inevitable . . . If these forebodings shall be realized, and a separation of the states shall occur, momentous considerations will be presented to the corporate authorities of this city. We must provide for the new relations which will necessarily grow out of the new condition of public affairs . . ."

Now for the proposal that would avenge him with the state legislature. *Take the police force away from me, will you!*

". . . The Legislature in which the present partisan majority has the power, has become the instrument by which we are plundered to enrich their speculators, lobby agents, and Abolitionists. Laws are passed through their malign influence, by which, under the forms of legal enactment, our burdens have been increased, our sustenance eaten out, and our municipal liberties destroyed . . . When disunion has become a fixed and certain fact why may not New York disrupt the bonds which bind her to a venal and corrupt master—to a people and a party that have plundered her revenues, attempted to ruin her commerce, taken away the power of self-government, and destroyed the Union of which she was the proud Empire City?"

Some were shocked. But not all. New York City—a free and independent city-state! It was a fascinating idea especially for New Yorkers of the mid-nineteenth century who thought of everything west of the Hudson as one big corn field.

And Wood was the hero of the hour. Already the regular Tammany organization had deserted him and he had been forced to form his own party—the Mozart Hall Democracy, he called it, after the building where they had their headquarters.

The regular Tammanyites were chagrined. Wood always managed to grab the headlines. He was always ready with the unexpected—the grand gesture. Anti-war feeling was strong in the North. Even Greeley cautioned reserve. "Let the erring sisters depart," he said, "in peace."

All over the country leading Democrats sent letters of praise to Wood for his stand—Fernando Wood, ex-grog-shop keeper, dealer in wickedness and devious ways. He seemed invincible. Some of the regular Tammany Hall Democrats advocated charging him with treason. Tweed killed that. Wait, he said. Everybody makes mistakes. Maybe this secession proposal is not the brilliant move that it seems.

Tweed was right. The tide turned. It was a slow turning and almost imperceptible. But it was there.

Mr. Lincoln was inaugurated in Washington, standing awkwardly tall under the unfinished dome of the capitol building.

". . . I hold that, in contemplation of universal law and of the Constitution, the Union of these States is perpetual. Perpetuity is implied, if not expressed, in the fundamental law of all national governments. It is safe to assert that no government proper ever had a provision in its organic law for its own termination. Continue to execute all the express provisions of our national Constitution, and the Union will endure forever—it being impossible to destroy it except by some action not provided for in the instrument itself."

The Honorable Mr. Wood had no answer to that. He didn't even try. One statement had come in conflict with another in the market place of ideas, and one would prove unworthy. Lincoln, of course, was not speaking of New York City. But he was speaking of Union, and echoes long-unheard were heard again. Abraham Lincoln and a crowd who stood there looking up at his homely, beautiful face. When he stood to speak, he removed his hat and looked around for a place to put it. Senator Douglas reached over and took it and held it, knowing perhaps at last, that words that he could never have said were being said.

". . . I am loath to close. We are not enemies but friends. We must not be enemies. Though passion may have strained, it must not break our bonds of affection. The mystic chords of memory, stretching from every battle-field and patriot grave to every living heart and hearthstone all over this broad land, will yet swell the chorus of the Union when again touched, as surely they will be, by the better angels of our nature."

Wood tried to climb on the bandwagon. Suddenly he was

intensely patriotic. And after the firing on Fort Sumter, he realized, belatedly, his mistake. Frantically almost, he summoned up words to speak that he hoped would drown out the memory of words he had written. For once, it wasn't a very good performance:

"And now, let me invoke my countrymen to a study of the example of Washington. We are in the midst of a revolution, more momentous, and yet not unlike that in which his glorious services were active. He fought to create a Republic: let us die, if need be, to maintain it . . . And would to God that the whole people—the men of every section which has derived so much advantage from the Union—could present but one front in this, the trying hour of its peril . . ."

Too late, Mr. Mayor. The regular Tammany Hall organization had unfurled a banner outside the Wigwam: "The Union must and shall be preserved." Andrew Jackson had said it first and it seemed that the shades of the old giants were with Tammany—with Tweed. Tammany also raised a regiment and sent it to the front. Wood bustled about getting a regiment of his own together.

It was too late. Tweed didn't really destroy Wood. Lincoln did. And without even trying. It was the words he said.

"In your hands, my dissatisfied fellow countrymen, and not in mine, is the momentous issue of civil war. The government will not assail you. You have no conflict without yourselves being the aggressors. You have no oath registered in heaven to destroy the government, while I shall have the most solemn one to 'preserve, protect, and defend it.' "

Wood had no oath registered in heaven about anything.

And he ran again for mayor. It was 1861. Tweed was candidate for sheriff that year. But he didn't care about the job, really. He wanted to expel Wood from city politics once and for all. There was still plenty of anti-war spirit in New York and the fight would be a tough one. Tweed spent

$100,000 on the campaign. This was his big chance and he knew it. Some damning figures were published. And this time Tweed didn't have to lie. Wood had stolen a quarter of a million dollars from the city. And the facts were clear. He had awarded a street-cleaning contract for $279,000 a year, for example, even though another contractor had offered to do the work for $84,000 less. Benjamin Wood had an interest in the company of the successful bidder.

Wood ran for re-election. And this time it was a real fight. Once, he said he could have committed a murder in his family and won election. But now he had stolen city money and even worse, the story was out.

In 1861 Election Day fell on a Wednesday, December 4th. It was a cold day and crispy. There were three candidates. The regular Tammany organization nominated C. Godfrey Gunther, a rich merchant who was supposed to deliver the German vote. The Republicans ran George Opdyke, also a merchant. He was conservative, well-liked, a little unsophisticated in the ways of ward politics.

The Mozart Hall Democracy, of course, nominated Wood.

Cold, that December Wednesday, and crispy. The *New York Times* called it a quiet election and it was, relatively. There were the usual fist fights. A gang of Wood supporters attacked two Opdyke men at a polling place at Tenth Avenue and Twenty-seventh Street and one of the gang was shot and killed. And down in the Sixth Ward, a man named Martin Waters was reckless enough to announce that he did not intend to vote for Wood. In attempting to dissuade him from his convictions, a Wood man struck him with a pistol butt and injured him seriously. Still, as the *Times* said, it was a relatively quiet day.

Barnum was exhibiting a live whale at his museum and the day before, the new President had sent a message to Congress: "The struggle of today is not only for today. It is

for a vast future also." War, and the talk of war. At Laura
Keene's Theater that night there was a patriotic musical
presented called *Seven Sons*. It included a number of
tableaux: "The Spirit of Jackson at the Tomb of Washington," "The Star of the Union," "North and South," "An
Episode at Valley Forge," "The Death of the Rebel Spy,"
and, for some reason, a scene involving "Arcadian nymphs
reclining among their flocks by a mountain torrent of real
water." It didn't have anything to do with the war, but it
was probably better than Barnum's whale.

The *New York Times* reprinted from the *Boston Christian
Advertiser* a quotation attributed to the Bible that must
have given comfort to Unionists: "Behold there shall be a
rebellion in the south, a rebellion of strong men and archers
of chariots and bright shields, and the blast of the trumpet
shall awaken the land, and the nations shall be astonished
thereat. And lo, behold, because of the sin of the south, her
mighty men shall be as babes, her gates shall be destroyed
utterly, saith the Lord, yea utterly destroyed shall be her
gates, and her rice fields shall be wasted and her slaves set
free."

It turned out to be a spurious quotation and the editors of
the *Times* were a little petulant about the retraction. At
least, they said, it had the salubrious effect of sending many
readers to search Bibles not frequently read.

A man who signed himself S.A.W. advertised for a second
lieutenant's commission "for which a reasonable price would
be paid."

And this in the *Herald:* "Personal: Sixth Avenue Car
Yesterday: Would the young lady who, in the company of
another young lady, got into a Sixth Avenue car about 5 P.M.
yesterday and who carried a small black dog, like to make
the acquaintance of the young man who stood in front of

her and who got out at 23rd street? Address J.B.W. Madison
Square Post Office, 945 Broadway."

There was an early darkness and the returns of the day's
voting began to come in. The best places to go were the
newspaper offices where bulletins were marked up with the
latest returns. But the various party headquarters were really
more exciting. The Republican headquarters was at 618
Broadway. You couldn't miss it. There was a huge banner
strung across the street with Opdyke's name on it. Thousands
jammed into the little building. A rumor spread that the
floor was giving way and everyone rushed to the street.
Opdyke arrived early, but the returns were inconclusive and
he left. Later, a great throng beating drums and carrying
torches marched up to his home on Fifth Avenue near Sixtieth Street. But he wasn't there and the demonstration
petered out.

At Tammany Hall it was clear that it was more important
to defeat Wood than to elect Gunther. The *Times* again
". . . above the din and cackle of the jabbering throng,
through the clouds of smoke and the all-pervading fumes of
whiskey, could be heard the constantly repeated declaration
that Wood was played out—'Wood's gone in,' 'Wood's nowhere,' D—n Wood!"

A speaker gets up on a chair and announces that he has
a right to speak to Democrats even though he had made a
fool of himself and voted for Abe Lincoln. A man who, the
Times reporter observed, had just borrowed six cents to get
a drink, offered to bet $500 to $200 that Gunther would win.

But the Opdyke votes were rolling in. Gunther was holding his own, but the Republicans were showing surprising
strength.

At Wood's Mozart Hall there was stunning news. The
Sixth Ward was deserting Wood! It was not yet time to
concede but already the shadows were forming. The Honor-

able D. B. Taylor, chairman for the occasion, did his best to make it a good party: "I feel it 'way back in the deepest recesses of my heart that Fernando Wood is elected."

There were cheers at that and Mr. Taylor went on, "It will be the most important event since the election of Linkhorn to the presidential chair."

Only a mild response to that—he'd have to do better.

"The party to which Mr. Opdyke belongs wants to make this a war for the extermination of the white man and the glorification of the nigger. They delight in the thought that the Negro is better than a white man. I only wish they would come out boldly and be compelled to hug the nigger wenches."

There was some cheering for that, but at Mozart Hall that night there was little enough to celebrate. As the evening pushed toward midnight, everyone knew. It was close, but Wood was through. He was out. He had finally ceased to be either compelling or amusing.

The final returns: Opdyke, 25,380; Gunther, 24,767; and Wood, 24,167. Tweed lost in his race for sheriff. But he was a very happy man that midnight. Wood was through! The road was clear. His destiny was manifest.

At Mozart Hall, Taylor goes to the speakers' platform again: "We will hope for the best, although I must confess it will be hoping against hope. We must now watch and think and contemplate and hope. We will now bring these proceedings to a close."

It was as good an epitaph as any on the career of Fernando Wood in New York City. For in truth, as far as New York was concerned, the proceedings were at a close.

Wood made an agreement with the regular Tammany organization. He would run for Congress. Oh, yes—one last thing. There were some people whom he wanted nominated

"The Tammany Hotel, owned by the Tammany Society, at Nassau and Frankfort Streets, held out. There is an advertisement in the papers calling attention to its 'salutary location, being on high and open ground and airy.' This was not entirely true but no one ventured to challenge the statement. No one really cared. Tammany was not yet the powerful organization it would become." Tammany Hall, 1830.

"New York's first gangs were bred in the dark and swampy slums of the Five Points." A Five Points gangster of the 1840's.

"They fought with the Five Pointers, plastered their hair with Batcheler's Celebrated Hair Dye and walked the streets as if they owned it." A Bowery B'hoy.

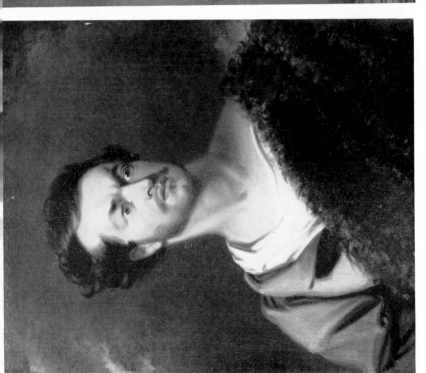

"In the late 1840's a feud developed between Edwin Forrest, the country's most popular actor, and William C. Macready, a very popular English actor." Macready, left, and Forrest, right, as Macbeth.

"St. John's Park . . . gas lit by night and by day jealously guarded by lovely old homes and nurses in uniforms and their proper children." St. John's Park, New York, in the 1840's.

"She . . . eventually built a huge mansion on Fifth Avenue and Fifty-second Street. 'Your house is built on babies' skulls,' the children would shout." The home of Madame Restell, notorious abortionist.

"The mayor of New York in 1857 was almost a distillation of all the weaknesses and strengths of the time and place." Fernando Wood, Mayor of New York and ex grog shop keeper.

"The job (of arresting Wood) fell to a hard-jawed, veteran policeman named Captain George W. Walling . . . Curiously enough he was allowed to enter City Hall and walk into the Mayor's office." Captain George W. Walling of the Metropolitan Police.

"Heat and propinquity and never quite enough to eat. Add leadership to this and a purpose, combine the gangs and take into their ranks all the other angry, hungry people and they can take over a city. They can take over any city. And they would take this one." The Dead Rabbits' Riot at Bayard and Elizabeth Streets, July 4, 1857.

"He thought big and looked big . . . a huge egg-shaped head and a waistline that showed the effects of too many roast duck and beef and oyster dinners . . . He looks a little like a shrewd and calculating Santa Claus." William Marcy Tweed, Grand Sachem of Tammany.

"Nast had gone far since the days when he studied English and arithmetic in that little school down on Chrystie Street . . . He was tough and courageous and he hated injustice and bullies. And he remembered being frightened by a bully back in school . . . a kid dressed in fireman's clothes." William Marcy Tweed as seen by Thomas Nast.

"*These jokes, these pompous allusions to the classics, they really hid a soaring ambition. But Hall didn't want money. He wanted recognition and fame and applause. Tweed could provide that in abundance.*" Abraham Oakey Hall, Mayor of New York City.

"*A man of vigor but also of sullen quietness. And he was constantly plotting. Indeed, his whole life seemed to be one giant conspiracy.*" Peter B. Sweeny, City Chamberlain.

"And they all lived together in a crooked little house."

"*The fact that no one seemed to trust Connolly disturbed Tweed not at all. Connolly had imagination and nerve. What's integrity? Tweed could find that in any bank clerk.*" Richard B. Connolly, Comptroller of the City of New York.

"'*What of that,' Judge Barnard answered. 'Do you think I can tell whether she has committed adultery by looking at her?*'" George G. Barnard, Justice of the New York Supreme Court.

"At a signal from Jenkins another clerk, Charles H. Carpenter, walked to the drum. He reached into the drum, withdrew a small piece of rolled-up paper, and passed it to Jenkins. Jenkins unrolled it and read: 'William Jones, 46 Street, corner Tenth Avenue.'" The draft begins in New York City, Saturday, July 11, 1863.

"A man detaches himself from the mob and climbs to the roof of a little shanty near Third Avenue. 'Organize,' (he) says, 'or otherwise you will be drafted. Lincoln wants to tear you from your home and send you to war. And although it's not generally known,' he tells the crowd, 'Lincoln is really a Negro himself.'" Draft Riot, July 13, 1863.

"*During the rest of the rioting police would be mildly shocked to find some of the mobsters dressed impeccably in Brooks Brothers suits.*" Looting of Brooks Brothers store on Catherine Street, July 14, 1863.

"*He was dragged to the street and, as the thunder muttered away and the sky lightened in the east, a noose was thrown around his neck and he was hanged.*" Hanging of William Jones of Clarkson Street, July 13, 1863.

"*The children were led through the back. The rioters splintered the door and swarmed inside. Somehow in the excitement of the escape one child had been left behind.*" Rioters carrying loot from the Colored Orphan Asylum at Fifth Avenue and 43rd Street, July 14, 1863.

"*For hours they played with him. They dragged him into his own backyard and turned him over to the women. They used knives first and then threw stones at his head. But it was evening before he died.*" Murder of Col. H. J. O'Brien of the Eleventh New York Volunteers, July 14, 1863.

"Five million dollars to lay off. Five million dollars, Mr. Jones. 'Why, with that you could go to Europe and live like a prince.' . . . 'Yes,' Jones said, 'I could live like a prince, but I would know that I was a rascal.' " George Jones, co-founder and editor of the *New York Times.*

"He might have led the fight instead of those fellows over at the Times. Everything they knew about the newspaper business they learned from him. But he missed this fight somehow." Horace Greeley, editor of the New York *Tribune.*

Photograph of Thomas Nast.

A famous Nast Cartoon.

WHO STOLE THE PEOPLE'S MONEY? — DO TELL . N.Y.TIMES.   'TWAS HIM.

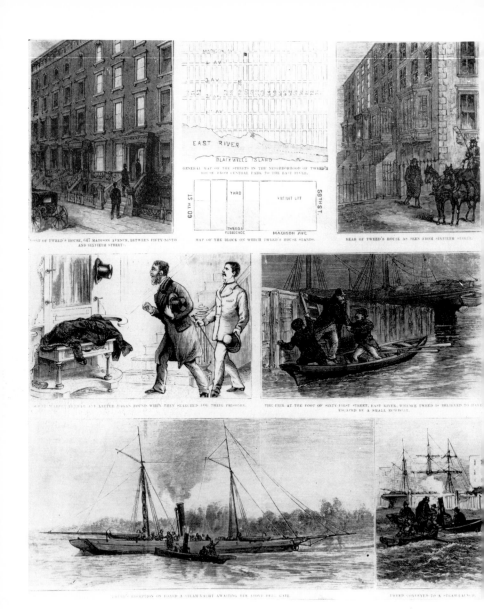

"Tweed had simply hurried out the back door to the street where a carriage was waiting. At a signal he jumped in and, by that gesture, he became a fugitive for whom there would be no rest until he died." Tweed escape scenes as published in Leslie's Weekly, Dec. 18, 1875.

to various city offices. In fact, there had been a financial arrangement and the money had been paid.

Tammany and Tweed were glad enough to pay this final debt. The money mentioned as paid to Wood was somewhere between $100,000 and $200,000.

Wood went to Congress as planned where he spent almost twenty undistinguished years. When he died in 1881, Representative Covert of New York delivered a eulogy on the floor of the House of Representatives:

"What shall I say of him whose presence was so familiar to us all in this chamber? Of him who, after nearly twenty years of faithful service in this House, has made his last appeal to us, and answered his last roll-call, and has passed out from this chamber, never to enter its portals?"

Then this, a quotation from Spenser:

"You knew—who knew not Astrophel?
Alas! That I should say I knew,
And have not in possession still!
Things known permit me to renew.
Of him you know his merit such
I cannot say . . . you hear . . . too much."

Wood had died in Hot Springs, Arkansas, where he had gone to recover from inflammatory pneumonia complicated by gout. An honor guard of congressmen left Washington to escort the body back to New York City. He was still remembered there. The *Herald* remembered: "In the lower wards of the city he was very popular, especially with the roughs, over whom he exercised almost limitless influence by reason of his temperance principles, habits of sobriety and self-control." And the writer pointed out that the late Mr. Wood used to read the *Herald* every morning.

Wood left an estate of over half a million dollars.

And he left his mark over the city. The Dead Rabbits were his as surely as if he had invented them. The city was dark with slums where there might have been cleanliness and pride. Poverty was his running mate. Who the master and who the slave? For one terrible week the issue was in doubt.

No one guessed that it would happen, but it did. Tweed didn't guess it, although he might have.

He probably did not think about it at all. It had all been pretty easy, after all. People were sheep, really. You can always frighten the timid and pay off the bold. And Tweed was doing fine. He was still a member of the Board of Supervisors and had become chairman of the Democratic Central Committee of New York County. Normally this wasn't a particularly impressive post. Tweed would make it very important. He controlled the Common Council. Let the Republican mayor veto any bill he wanted. Tweed would simply speak a few words, make a few promises and the councilmen would override any veto. Like the bill to pay a bonus of $200 to newspapermen assigned to cover City Hall and the higher courts. Mayor Opdyke was shocked. The implication was obvious. He would never sign such a bill.

Tweed didn't expect that he would. He spoke to some of the Council members and told them to pass the word along. The bill passed. Later newspapers and newspapermen would get even a better break. Tweed simply created city jobs with good pay and no work involved and awarded them to anyone with press credentials. In fact, there is some indication that a large number of persons were handed these sinecures simply on their own statement that they were reporters. Tweed didn't have the time to check the facts and he couldn't afford to take chances.

And, on the part of newspapers, there were practical reasons for establishing cordial relations with City Hall.

Public auctions were advertised, notices of bankruptcy and so forth. Tweed would turn this into a device for insuring a good press. When the military draft law was passed, for example, Tammany had all the names of prospective draftees printed. It was a tidy bit of income for the publishers. And, of course, the city paid. Volumes of unimportant and routine city matters were duly sent to various newspapers and no bill rendered the city was ever challenged. A paper called the *Transcript* carried practically no other advertising and did very well financially. In one five year period, it billed the city for a total of $783,498.09, and the *Daily News*—no connection with the present *New York Daily News*—received $489,980.67. Their columns, of course, were always available to Tweed for whatever press release he might want to write and any news stories that reflected unfavorably on the city administration simply did not appear. In that same period, the *Herald* got $91,491.88 from city advertising. And about a dozen or so *Herald* reporters were city employees with no duties, of course, except to pick up a weekly pay check. Even *The Times* at first got a little cut out of the pie—$75,160.08 in five years.

And Tweed's affairs went merrily along. There was a public auction of benches rendered inappropriate when Harlem Hall was turned into a church. Tweed, in his official position on the Committee on Armories in the Board of Supervisors, bought three hundred of the benches at $5.00 each. Most of these were turned over to the furniture house of Ingersoll and Company which was owned by a man who had started out as a chairmaker with old Richard Tweed.

The benches were later sold back to the city for $600.00 each—a total bill of $169,800. Some of the steal must have gone to others, but Tweed got a large portion. It would not take him long to make back that $100,000 he spent defeating Wood.

And the city was growing bigger and richer every day. The war was dreadful, of course, and these damned Republicans will be the ruin of the country one day. But the war did present possibilities for anyone interested in the manipulation of money.

Not so for the disenchanted down in the Five Points. By 1863, the costs of living had doubled what they were two years before. Flour prices had soared. Roast beef, which had sold for eight cents a pound in 1861, now was priced at sixteen cents a pound. Eggs had more than doubled—from twelve and a half cents for thirteen to twenty-five cents a dozen.

And work was hard to get. Three men for every job. It was the Negroes the Irish immigrants said. They'll work for nothing. And if the Republicans win this war and free the slaves, they'll all come to New York and nobody will have a job. Maybe we'll even have to work for them.

There had been hints of what was coming. The riot of the Dead Rabbits and the Bowery Boys on that Fourth of July, 1857, had been one. And there were more now. Increased fighting along the docks where the Irish workers and the Negroes competed for jobs. And in the winter of 1863, there were a number of suspicious fires in the shacks in the Negro areas around the Five Points. They should have known, those in authority. The police seemed to know and gave warnings. But no one listened. There had always been slums in New York.

It was true. There had long been slums. Rynders and Wood and Tweed did not invent them. There had long been hungry men in New York who walked the streets in bitterness. What Tammany had done was to give them leadership and a sense of importance. They had taught them contempt of the voting laws and, by extension, all laws. Tammany had taught them to hate the rich. They had bartered in resentment and nursed anger and self-pity as political weapons.

On March 3, 1863, President Lincoln signed what was called the National Conscription Act. It provided for the enrollment of all males between the ages of eighteen and forty-five. Quotas were set up for each city and state. These were not made public, but it was understood that 12,500 men were to be drafted from New York City. The Democrat newspapers were quick to react. They published editorials attacking the administration and some even carried advertisements blatantly promising advice on how to avoid the draft. Cost—one dollar.

The editorial page lent aid and comfort to the advertisers. The law, editors wrote, was designed to punish the poor and protect the rich. And it was a good argument. Any man could be excused from the draft if he paid the government three hundred dollars. That was a fortune down on the Bowery or the miserable little streets that lined the East Side. Or, if you wished, you could buy a substitute and have him appear in your place. *Buy* one! It was a plot, some were saying. Only Democrats will be drafted. It's a plot to keep the Republicans in power forever.

Fires in the Negro areas and an increasing number of fights. That's the way it was all spring and into the summer. They might have guessed—Tweed and the others. They did not.

In June of that year, Lee had moved north into Pennsylvania with three corps, and President Lincoln had sent an emergency call to New York, Pennsylvania, West Virginia and Maryland, for 120,000 soldiers to help stem the tide. New York and Brooklyn responded promptly with seventeen regiments. The Republican papers applauded this. But no one seemed to notice that it left the biggest city in the country practically devoid of troops. There were some men of the Invalid Corps on guard duty, a few National Guard and volunteer units, the crews of Navy vessels in port, and the garrisons of the city forts—less than two thousand men.

Saturday, July 11th. Lee had been soundly thrashed near the little market town of Gettysburg in Pennsylvania and Vicksburg had fallen to Union besiegers. But the war was not over. Maybe, they were saying down in the Five Points, the Republicans don't want it to be over.

Saturday, July 11, 1863. The first selection of names in New York City was set for that day. There were two offices: one at 1190 Broadway near Twenty-ninth Street; another at 677 Third Avenue near the corner of Forty-sixth Street. The Saturday drawing was in the office at Third Avenue.

It began shortly after nine in the morning. The room was filled with men, many of them potential draftees. Provost Marshall Charles Jenkins, in charge of the conscription there, surveyed the crowd and noted that, while the men were loud and boisterous, they did not seem to be in a dangerous mood. He was a little relieved. There had been some violence in a few areas in western states at the drawing of names. Jenkins read the Conscription Act to the crowd. There was a lot of joking. You couldn't really hear much of what he was saying.

When he was through an assistant, George W. Southwick, turned a huge drum in which the enrolled names had been placed. They waited in silence for it to stop. Jenkins waited. There were crossed flags above his head. At a signal from Jenkins, another clerk, Charles H. Carpenter, walked to the drum. Carpenter was blindfolded and his right sleeve was turned up. He reached into the drum, withdrew a small piece of rolled-up paper and passed it to Jenkins. Jenkins unrolled it and read:

"William Jones, Forty-sixth Street, corner Tenth Avenue."

Jones was present. He was surrounded by laughing, joking men who slapped him on the back and raised his right hand into the air. "Our Willie's gone to be a soldier!"—"Good-by, Willie" . . . There was more. Jenkins watched closely. This wasn't bad at all. The draft had gone well in a couple of New England states. Maybe it would go peaceably here, too.

And other names were called—1,236 altogether. Everyone cheered and laughed when City Councilman Joyce's name was pulled out. Six of the enrolling officers of the district were called. And there was a man named Mother Cull who lived at 529 West Forty-sixth Street. There was laughter about that. There was a lot of laughter there that day.

At six o'clock the drawing was called off until Monday morning. Not bad. Some grumbling, they said, among the crowd that milled around outside. But no worse than what might have been expected. And there'll be a weekend now for things to simmer down.

Sunday dawn was hot and sultry and it would stay that way all day. Governor Horatio Seymour, a Democrat, had stopped by briefly to inspect the city's defenses and had taken off quickly for a holiday at Long Branch, New Jersey. Mayor Opdyke was at home. Hot, sultry, and not a breath of wind. In Central Park, people climbed to the top of the Observatory, but there was no breeze even there.

There were hints. A reporter for the *Herald* was given the assignment of walking through the Twentieth Ward where yesterday's drawing had taken place to test the temper of those who lived there. The *Herald* that Sunday had printed the names of the draftees and everyone seemed to have a copy. He heard one man: "If Lincoln attempts to enforce the draft in New York, there will be black eyes and bloody noses." And in a tavern he listened carefully to a man who was sounding off to the others: "Let them come on, and I will resist the whole draft myself." The speaker, he noted, had downed three brandies and two "gin cocktails."

Down at police headquarters at 300 Mulberry Street, it looked like a fairly routine evening. The city, perhaps, was a little restless and there seemed to be an unusual number of people on the streets even at the late hours. Probably the heat. Detectives sent in their reports . . . some indication that the Copperhead Knights of the Golden Circle planned to seize the Arsenal at Seventh Avenue and Thirty-fifth Street in protest to the draft. In the Eighth Ward there is a workingman's group being organized to resist the draft . . .

That was all. Looking back on it now it seems as if that should have been enough. But no one thought much about it on that night or in the early hours of Monday, July 13th.

Thunder and the threat of rain. Slowly, reluctantly, most of the city went to bed.

But not all. Many stayed up that night. The taverns were crowded. It was the heat. And the damned draft.

We should do something about it, they were saying . . .

CHAPTER 6

REAP THE WHIRLWIND

"They have sown the wind, and they shall reap the whirlwind."
— Hosea. 8: 7.

It STARTED EARLY MONDAY MORNING. Some of them probably did not sleep at all. At dawn there were small groups of men on the street corners of the Bowery and Five Points and the little streets that ran east to the river. The groups became bigger and their voices louder and as their voices rose so did their anger. Slowly they began to move. West first to Sixth Avenue and then north. They filled the streets. Some of them were armed. You could hear them before you could see them. You could hear the shouts of those who were taking command. And you could hear their feet against the cobbled streets. And that was the most frightening of all. They walked in the streets, filling them. And then they grew and spilled over onto the sidewalks. Wherever there was a factory, some of them would dash inside and order everyone out. Join us, they said, or take the consequences. Most would join.

And so they grew and moved like a tide. North to Fourteenth Street—Thirty-fourth—Forty-second . . . One observer timed one mob that surged through a side street. It took

125

them about twenty-five minutes to pass a point. But no one could count their numbers. It was in the thousands.

They gathered finally in an open, vacant area near Central Park. Already there was a plan. And there was leadership. There was even a certain amount of discipline. They formed into two groups and started downtown again, one group marching along Fifth Avenue, the other taking over Sixth Avenue. No violence yet. But you could see their weapons— axes, clubs—a few carried firearms. And there were placards. NO DRAFT one of them read.

At Forty-sixth Street they turned to their left and headed for the enrollment office. As they crossed Fourth (now Park) Avenue, squads detached themselves from the main body and cut down the telegraph lines that bordered the tracks of the Harlem and New Haven Railroad.

In the enrollment office on Forty-sixth Street, Provost Marshall Jenkins was preparing to select the names that would complete the quota in that district. There was a squad of policemen on duty in case of trouble—later in the morning they were reinforced—sixty patrolmen all together. Most were outside the building, but a few were in the big room with the revolving drum and the crossed flags. At Police Headquarters down at 300 Mulberry Street, an order is telegraphed to all police stations in New York and Brooklyn: "Call in your reserves. Platoon them and hold them at the station houses subject to further orders." And in the little building on Forty-sixth Street, the draft starts again.

It sounded like a storm at first. It was almost like a rising wind or a heavy surf. It was their voices and the sound of their feet. They were coming across Forty-sixth Street. A mob. The street is black with them. They want to stop the draft.

Jenkins orders the drum to be turned. The police form outside, protecting the doors. They might as well have tried to hold back the turning of the tide. The mob had arrived. And they kept pressing closer and closer.

Then there was a shot. It was a signal for a rush. And the mob rolled forward. It was ten-thirty.

The police fought well, cracking down with their clubs. It was futile. For every man felled, there were a hundred more. The police were forced back into the buildings. They closed the door and bolted it. But it was too late. A shower of bricks and paving stones slammed against the outside walls. Windows splintered and even above the roar of the mob, you could hear the tinkle of glass across the floor.

Jenkins, his assistants and the police managed to escape by a rear door. Just in time. The mob burst in.

Upstairs, a few families who lived in the building listened in terror to what was going on below. A member of the mob, his face flushed, bangs on the door and tells them to get out. This building is going to be burned. They got out. But just in time. There were flames licking at the wood on the lower floors. In a short time the whole building was aflame. A volunteer fire company answered the alarm but the mob would not let them unlimber their hoses. They just sat there and watched. The enrollment office burned first and then three buildings adjoining.

It might have ended there. The mob had accomplished its purpose. There would be no more draft. At least, not then and, at least, not there.

It didn't end there. They had tasted blood. Three buildings across the street were set afire also. This was pointless. And there would be more.

A man detaches himself from the mob and climbs to the roof of a little shanty near Third Avenue. And he begins to speak. "You must," he says, "organize to resist the draft." And he offers to be their leader. A reporter for the *Tribune* scribbles down with shaking hands what he can find out about the speaker. He is a Mr. Andrews from Virginia. He has a beard and a red shirt. That's all he can find out about him. It's all anyone ever found out. "Organize," says Mr. Andrews—or otherwise you will be drafted. Lincoln wants to tear you from your home and send you to war. And although it's not generally known, Andrews tells the crowd, Lincoln is really a Negro himself.

The three buildings across the avenue from the enrollment office were burning fiercely now. But this did not satiate the crowd. Other buildings must be burned. Let the rich people suffer for once. Burn more. Burn them all down . . .

A detachment from the Invalid Corps was dispatched to the scene. They came marching up Third Avenue, their rifles at right shoulder arms. They marched briskly. Each of them had been wounded in the war. Some limped. But they moved with the steadiness of veterans.

Not for long. The mob was told of their coming and thousands swept downtown to meet them. The meeting came at Forty-second Street. There was a shower of stones and some of the veterans dropped. Their officer ordered half of the number to fire. The guns were loaded with blanks except for one rank. Six of the mobsters were hit. Three were killed outright. But the mob pressed on. The soldiers were overwhelmed. The rifles were wrested from their hands and used as clubs against them.

The soldiers turned and fled. The mob cheered and made obscene gestures at their backs.

Three who had stayed too long were not allowed to escape. Two of them were beaten to death with their rifle butts. A third ran east toward the river. It was a mistake. He found himself on a high cliff with the mob behind him and a sharp drop ahead. He might as well have been trapped in one of the dead end streets of the Five Points. The mob caught him and threw him down to the rocks below. Then they hurled huge boulders down on top of him. And there he died.

At eleven-fifteen an order went out to close all draft offices throughout the city.

It was too late. Another mob had formed downtown. They swarmed through all factories and workshops and shipyards and ordered everyone off the job. Most went home. Some stayed to watch the excitement. A few joined the mobs.

Transportation was next. All cars on Second and Third Avenues were halted quickly by the mobs. The railroads stopped running at noon. And the telegraph wires leading into Police Headquarters were cut. By one in the afternoon, all but two of the main police wires had been cut. The two that functioned were secret wires. The mobs never found them and they remained operating all through the dreadful days that followed.

Mayor Opdyke hastily summoned a special meeting of the Common Council. Less than a half a dozen answered the call. And without a quorum present, they could do nothing. Mobs swarming around the Park in front of City Hall. There were police there, too. But the mobs were growing bolder. They were right under the Mayor's window. He could see their weapons waving in the air. He moved his office to the St. Nicholas Hotel on Broadway at Spring Street.

The city's ranking police officer, Superintendent John A. Kennedy, read the early dispatches that came in, jumped into a carriage and, still not realizing the extent of the riot, headed for Forty-sixth Street. He was in civilian clothes and carried a light bamboo cane. He dismounted at Forty-sixth Street and Lexington Avenue and headed for Third Avenue. He never made it. He was half way down the block when someone in the crowd recognized him and shouted his name. Instantly he was surrounded by a ring of angry, distorted faces. And one of the mob stepped forward and knocked him to the street. His assailant wore an old army uniform. Kennedy scrambled to his feet and slashed his attacker with his cane. But it was a fragile weapon and they had numbers. Again he was knocked down, kicked and stomped on. He managed to gain his feet and started to run back to Lexington Avenue. He stumbled, cut and bleeding, into the arms of a man named John Eagen who was well known in the neighborhood. Eagen convinced the mob that Kennedy was dead and, exulting in their triumph, they turned back to the scene of the fires.

Kennedy was hastily loaded onto a wagon, covered with some old sacks and driven back to Headquarters. He was not dead but almost. A surgeon examined him and later said that he found seventy-two bruises on his body and some twenty cuts. Hospitalized, his command fell then on two men: Commissioners John C. Bergen, who was in charge of Brooklyn and Staten Island, and Thomas C. Acton, who would direct police actions in Manhattan. For Acton, at least, this was the day that would forever divide the old from the new, and he handled himself and his force superbly.

Another mob swarmed down on the enrollment office at Broadway and Twenty-ninth Street. There was a jeweler's office in the same building. It was broken into and looted while a huge crowd watched. Not all bystanders were in sympathy with the mob. One man spoke out loudly: "This is an unspeakable outrage. As an American citizen I am ashamed." He might have had more to say, but his skull was laid open by one vicious blow from a club. And the looting went on.

Then someone started it and the word spread from mouth to mouth across the crowd. It was almost a chant. To the Armory they were saying. The building was on Second Avenue at Twenty-first Street. It was a four-story building, square and unpretentious and suddenly the most important building in the city. In the rooms on the top floors, guns and ammunition had been stored to await the disposition of the military. There were four thousand carbines there and about two hundred thousand rounds of ammunition.

To the Armory—to the Armory. Everyone whispered it until the sound became deafening and hugely portentious.

The police caught the words, of course, and dispatched a detail to guard it. There were thirty-two men. They covered the windows and the doors and they waited. It was two thirty when the mob appeared and swarmed around in the street outside. Many carried firearms which were readily available in those times. For an hour, the mob contented themselves with hurling bricks against the doors and windows and firing at the police whenever they showed themselves. The windows were broken. The street was littered with the stones they threw, but the munitions were safe.

The mob knew they would have to attack. It took them until four o'clock to summon up the courage and then they rushed the door. Their leader carried a sledge hammer. He managed to reach the door which he pounded with terrific blows.

One panel of the door broke open and a member of the mob, eager for distinction, rushed forward and forced his way through. A policeman inside shot him through the head. He was apparently well known down in the Five Points, but his name has not survived and the distinction he sought did not last the day.

Others followed him. They hammered at the door, using crowbars and even tree trunks. And they got in. For a few minutes the fighting was intense. But the police, knowing they could not stand off the thousands that crowded forward, retreated to the back of the building. Now all they could hope for was escape. There was a small hole in the rear wall that had not been discovered by the rioters. It was about twelve by eighteen inches, and every policeman in the building was over six feet tall. But they managed to squeeze through and drop eighteen feet to the ground. They clubbed their way through a small crowd that tried to stop them and fled to the station house of the Eighteenth Precinct, a block north and across toward Third Avenue. It was a fragile sanctuary. Within an hour the mob attacked here too and set the building on fire. Again there was an escape, and, weary and angered by defeat, the policemen finally managed to climb up the steps at Police Headquarters on Mulberry Street for gulps of hot coffee and a little rest.

The mob had a free hand at the Armory. And they found the carbines. Some broke open windows and tossed them by the armloads to the crowd below. Then boxes of ammunition crashed on the street and broke open. Now there would be heavy firing from both sides. Someone barricaded the door to the upstairs room where the guns were stored. It was a tragic error and ghastly in its result. New detachments of police arrived and, forcing their way through the mob, began to clear the building. And, of course, it was set on fire. The flames licked upward toward the room where a huge crowd was still breaking open the cases of guns. Suddenly—a wisp of smoke. They rushed to the door and clawed at the barricade. When finally they burst it open, it was too late. Some jumped from the windows and died that way. Later, when the riots were over and the building was being repaired and cleared of debris, workmen carried out more than fifty baskets and barrels of human bones. The bones were buried at Potter's Field.

By late afternoon, the rioting had taken on a new dimension. What had started out as a massive resistance to an unfair draft became something else. It became whatever the rioters wanted it to be. That meant stealing for some; fighting the hated police to others; and, for still others, a chance to attack Negroes in the name of suffering humanity. The police were deluged with reports of attacks on Negro communities across the city. No building where a Negro family lived was safe from attack and individuals caught by the mob were beaten and in some cases killed. The women, they would say later, were the worst. By dusk, there were three Negroes hanging from trees in separate places across the city.

And a crowd had gathered in front of the big frame building that sat back from Fifth Avenue at Forty-third Street. It was the Colored Orphan Asylum. There were two hundred Negro children there, all of them under twelve. And there was a staff of fifty adults. The Superintendent, William E. Davies, watched nervously as the crowd began to gather. It wasn't a mob yet. Just a crowd. But they were angry. They were yelling things. Nasty, ugly words. Davies barricaded the big front door and the crowd grew angrier. There were a few stones thrown. But they didn't move. Not yet.

Then, more trouble. A large mob had gathered to storm the Mayor's home at Fifth Avenue near Sixtieth. But his neighbors, under the command of a colonel, had taken precautions and the mob faced a quietly determined group, well armed, and obviously unafraid. Slowly and sullenly they withdrew and rolled back downtown. And here they met the crowd that was standing outside the Asylum. And as they grew larger in numbers, they grew louder, each urging his neighbor to action. Davies peered at the crowd through the window and gave the order to assemble all the children. Even as they lined up, the first of the rioters had jumped the little front wall and was pounding on the big front door. The children were led out through the back to Madison Avenue and hurried to the Twenty-second Precinct Station House on Forty-seventh Street between Eighth and Ninth Avenues. It was about five o'clock.

They made it just in time. The rioters splintered the door and swarmed inside. Nothing much there. A dining hall—

sleeping quarters. Toys and some books. But it wasn't entirely futile. Somehow, in the excitement of the escape, one child had been left behind. It was a little girl. They found her hiding under a bed. They killed her.

Darkness brought no respite. It brought long lines of refugees moving furtively out of the city. Some rode. Most of them walked. Boats unused for years were pressed into service. You could earn a fortune rowing families across the Hudson. They had to leave. The world had gone mad.

Night came and still the mobs swarmed through the streets. Many had died during the day, but there seemed to be more of them than ever before. Detectives, dressed like workmen, joined some of the mobs, walked with them and drank their fiery whiskey, and, at enormous risk, sent off secret messages to Headquarters of the plans that were being hatched. There were fires all across the city and even when you could not hear the voices you could smell the smoke. And it was getting worse. In some wards, many of the firemen were marching with the mobs; throughout the city, the rioters were attacking any firemen who dared to respond to the alarms. The worst was downtown. The Negro sections of the Five Points. The fires were spreading. Soon the rioters would be defeating their own purpose. Their own hovels would be burning, too. It was the time to stop. But the riot had a momentum of its own and it would never stop until it was put down.

More houses were set on fire that night. You could see the sullen glow against the clouds. Let a brisk wind come up and the whole city would be aflame.

But there was no wind. And the day's story had an almost Old Testament ending. It came shortly after eleven o'clock— rain. It began with a few splattering drops and turned into a downpour. It beat down on the hot streets and turned to steam. It filled the gutters. And then it came down harder still as though to cleanse the city of the day's debris. Rain beating down on the charred ruins of the draft office on Third Avenue. Rain coming through the broken windows of the Colored Orphan Asylum, deserted now and silent. And it put out the fires. There were great bellows of steam where a short time before there had been flame and smoke. And the big drops, insistent and chastising, dispelled the mobs more efficiently than had the blows of the policemen's nightsticks. Both sides were weary and went home for the night . . .

But both sides knew that the game would resume the next day. The police mustered their forces. They could count on fifteen hundred men. Policemen on vacation and special duty had reported in by the scores when the news came. The National Guard had been called out and had been joined by as many regular soldiers and Marines as could be spared from the forts around the city. There were about two thousand of these. Citizens, some of them veterans of the war, enlisted as volunteer special police and were issued identification. And everybody waited for the dawn.

And some started even before the dawn. It was still dark when, on Tuesday morning, a crowd surged through Clarkson Street which ran from Hudson Street past the old Trinity Parish Cemetery to the river. In 1863, it was largely a Negro neighborhood. Most of the Negroes had fled. But some stayed, and one tried to defend his home against the mob. He was dragged to the street and, as the thunder muttered away and the sky lightened in the east, a noose was thrown around his neck and he was hanged. A fire was built under his body and some of the crowd danced around it. The victim was named William Jones, by coincidence the name of the first man to be drafted the Saturday before. Probably no one knew it. Certainly no one cared. They cheered and laughed and made jokes about William Jones. The storm of last night had ended. It was a beautiful morning.

Governor Seymour arrived in town that afternoon. Tweed was there to meet him. So were some of the others from Tammany. The Governor's face was ashen when he stepped off the ferry. From the river you could see the work of the mobs. Smoke. Smoke over everything. Boatloads of refugees escaping the city. At the dock they shake hands and talk briefly. Each speaks in vapid and weary clichés. None dares to speak the truth. *Teach them to hold election laws in contempt and they will hold all laws in contempt. Teach them violence and they will recite their lessons back to you. Teach them to hate the rich and they will hate both the rich and the poor.* They rode in a carriage up Broadway to the Mayor's temporary headquarters at the St. Nicholas Hotel. On the way north, they passed several mobs. And they were recognized. There were cheers for the Governor. Cheers, too, for Tweed.

There's a hurried conference with the Mayor. The reports coming in from the various police precincts are dire and portentious. Word went out that the Governor would speak from the steps of City Hall.

A huge crowd gathered. They filled the little park in front and spilled out onto Broadway. They stood silent and waiting. Many of them were bloodied. Some wore bandages. But they would listen to the Governor. Only last Saturday he had warned the government that the draft should be suspended. They would listen to him.

The Governor came out and stood at the top of the steps. Tweed was standing by his side. Counselor-at-Law Tweed, he calls himself. And no one cares to question his right to the title. Judge Barnard had proclaimed it. He is fat and pompous. But he is not afraid. Governor Seymour is afraid. You can tell by the whiteness of his face. And his hands

shake. Tweed's hands are steady. Sheep, all of them. Tweed
was not afraid. That's not the way he played things. Let other
people be afraid of him. He smiles down at the mob and only
half listens to the Governor. He knows what the words
will be.

The Governor begins. His voice is strained and unnatural:

"I come, not only for the purpose of maintaining law, but
also from a kind regard for the interest and welfare of those
who, under the influence of excitement and a feeling of
supposed wrong, were in danger not only of inflicting serious
blows to the good order of society, but to their own interests.
I beg of you to listen to me as your friend and the friend of
your families."

Not all the Governor's friends were there that day. Some
were gathering at Second Avenue in front of the Union
Steam Works. It was just one block north of the Armory,
blackened and smelling of wet charcoal. And like the Armory, it was used for storing guns and ammunition. Others
of the Governor's friends were on Ninth Avenue. They were
building a street barricade, perhaps the most extensive in
the history of street-fighting in America. It extended from
Twenty-fourth Street to Forty-first Street. There were smaller
barricades across the intersecting streets. These people missed
the Governor's speech. It was a short one, considering the
intensity of the moment. He had come, he went on, to give
the people a test of his friendship. He was against the draft.

There were cheers and he left. Later he issued a proclamation: "The right of every citizen to make an appeal will be
maintained . . ."

The mobs neither knew about this nor cared. There were
those in the crowd who were saying that soon they would
control the city. Then they would make the proclamations.
Meanwhile, there was some work to be done.

Even as William Jones was being dragged across the still

wet stones of Clarkson Street, a mob was forming again at
the Union Steam Works. The police had been unable to remove the munitions there and the mob wanted them. A
thousand men gathered in the street before the building—
two thousand. The side streets were filled as others swarmed
down on the area.

At Police Headquarters, an inspector named Daniel Carpenter mustered a force of two hundred men and marched
double time to Second Avenue and then north to Twenty-
second Street. They could hear the mob before they could
see them. They could tell by the sound that it was a big mob
and angry. But they weren't quite prepared for what they
saw as they trotted up toward Twenty-second Street. The
whole avenue was filled with people. They stretched across
the street and up on the sidewalks. You could see their weapons. And there were thousands of them. Back they stretched
like some grotesque, seething reptile. The front of the crea-
ture was at Twenty-second Street; the tail was at Thirty-
third Street.

The police attacked.

They moved as skirmishers. They moved slowly but with
a certain inevitability. Some of the mob opened fire, but
their aim was poor. Stones fell about the police. Members of
the mob had infiltrated the houses on both sides of the street.
They threw things down on the police from rooftops, but
the men kept moving. And, just as slowly, the mob retreated.
Some hurried down side streets and re-formed behind the
police. At Thirty-second Street the mob halted its sullen
retreat and moved to the attack. A second attack rolled up
from the rear. The police stood their ground, using their
nightsticks against all who came within their reach. After
fifteen minutes of intense fighting, the mob, almost incredibly, broke off the fight and scurried for cover.

And for the police, help was near. News of the battle had

come to the Seventh Avenue Arsenal where a number of soldiers from various units were standing by. A hundred and fifty men were hastily formed outside and, under the command of Colonel H. J. O'Brien of the Eleventh New York Volunteers, started for the scene. They had two six-pound cannon and twenty-five experienced artillery men. As they approached the mob, Colonel O'Brien ordered his troops into company front. The artillery was wheeled into position and an order given to fire. The six-pounders fired grape and canister, and they were aimed into the very center of the mob.

No one knows how many were killed and wounded. But the street was dark with their bodies. Another round was fired. And another. There were six rounds fired, altogether. And the mob fell back. One of those killed was a woman with a baby in her arms. The woman fell with her body over the baby. She was fearfully trampled as the mob retreated, but the baby survived.

The mob was dispersed. A small body of policemen was detailed to guard the steam works. Second Avenue was quiet. But all over the city the rioters told of the fight. The soldiers. They had fired artillery to save themselves. Six times they had fired. Women had been killed—one of them with a baby. The story spread across the city. And it grew with the telling. Colonel O'Brien was in charge. He was the man who had given the order. Colonel O'Brien. Let's remember that name.

Colonel O'Brien marched the troops back to the Arsenal. Then he decided on a personal mission. His own home was not far from the scene of the morning's fighting and he was worried about the safety of his family. He went home. His family was safe. They had hurried off to Brooklyn before the fighting had begun. The Colonel was relieved. He turned his horse into Second Avenue and started back toward the Arsenal.

Sullen faces along the sidewalks and little knots of men standing in the brick-strewn street. Someone recognized him and shouted his name: Colonel O'Brien—he uses cannon against women. Someone grabbed at his leg and tried to pull him from his horse. Others formed a ring around him. There was a shower of stones. O'Brien reined in his horse and dismounted. He entered a saloon on the corner of Nineteenth Street. Maybe a patrol would come along and he could signal them. No patrol came. Stones slammed against the saloon door. The bartender suggested that he leave.

There was a big crowd now at the door. Colonel O'Brien walked out into the sunlight and drew his sword. For a moment the crowd was cowed by his courage and arrogance. But not for long. He took a few strides before one of them got close enough to strike him down with a club. He never got to his feet again. Like ants who have discovered a fallen delicacy, they swarmed down upon him. He was fearfully beaten and a rope twisted around his ankles. Then he was dragged back and forth across the cobblestones. At one point a priest came and held back the crowd long enough to administer the last rites. But the crowd was impatient and O'Brien not yet dead. For hours they played with him. And still he held on to life. They could see his lips moving and a sporadic movement of his head. They dragged him into his own backyard and turned him over to the women. They used knives first and then threw stones at his head. But it was evening before he died.

Another mob re-formed meanwhile and attacked the defenders of the Union Steam Works. This time they got in. They garrisoned the plant with about five hundred men. The plan was clear. This would serve as a headquarters for the mob. It was an excellent idea.

There were no historians for the mob. No one knows who their leaders were. In this battle, command seemed to be given to a giant who led the attacks and rushed upon the police with a huge bludgeon. The picture we have of him is vague. No one knows his name. No one knows where he lived or worked. A big fellow who worked as a night watchman or sold oysters from a cart. And maybe people liked him. But this day he was the embodiment of fury and hate. He had only one arm. And he was shot that day and killed.

One other person of all the thousands of the mob was remembered. He was a young man, roughly dressed as were all the mobsters. He had a knife and a club and he fought well, always in the vanguard when the mob and the police made contact. He became a special target and finally was struck down by a tremendous blow from a nightstick. He fell against an iron railing and was impaled on one of the stakes. In a lull in the fighting, police examined the body. He had been a member of the mob but not of them. His hands were unmarked by labor and well cared for. His skin was white and not tanned around the neck and arms like the others who worked out of doors. And his dirty overalls and filthy shirt were simply a disguise put on for reasons that no one will ever know. Beneath the working man's clothes were fine cashmere pants, a handsome and expensive vest and a linen shirt. He died there on Second Avenue and Twenty-second Street, fighting for a mob and probably no one will ever know what strange factors impelled him to that place at that time. The rioters managed to get his body and it was taken away. The story persisted that it was taken down to the Five Points and buried in one of the underground tunnels that honeycombed the area.

The mob did not hold the Union Steam Works for long. A detachment of two hundred police returned later in the day and, foot by foot, almost inch by inch, cleared the building. And this time the carbines and ammunition were loaded into wagons and taken to Police Headquarters.

Headquarters was a busy place that day. Reports were coming in from all over the city. The Weehawken Ferry House was on fire and heavy fighting going on at the barricades on Ninth Avenue.

All normal police activity was suspended, of course, but there is on record one fragile incident not connected with the riot. At one twelve that afternoon a telegram was sent to the police of the Fifth Precinct: "Send to Dr. Purple at 183 Hudson Street to go as soon as possible to Inspector Leonard's house. Baby very sick." An escort was provided for the doctor and he got there in time. The baby survived.

And the dispatches kept pouring in. A fourth attack had been launched against Greeley's *Tribune.* It was beaten off like all the others. A Negro church was set afire on Thirtieth Street between Seventh and Eighth Avenues. A lot of looting went on throughout the city. Sometime between eight and nine o'clock that night, a telegram warned that a large crowd was threatening to burn the Brooks Brothers Clothing Store which was then on Catherine Street. Police arrived to find the store already in flames and the merchandise thrown about the street. During the rest of the rioting, police would be mildly shocked to find some of the mobsters dressed impeccably in Brooks Brothers suits. Ultimately $10,000 worth of clothing was recovered, most of it hidden in the Five Points. In one shanty they found fifty suits.

Fires across the city and the sound of the mobs. The Governor issued a proclamation stating that a state of insurrection existed in the city. The mob had attacked a livery stable and some of them appeared on horses. The word spread swiftly across the city. The mob has cavalry. But it did them little good. The horses were not used to mobs and the riders could not control them. The rioters' cannon were also ineffective. There was no ammunition that would fit. The auxiliary police grew during the day, freeing more and more police and military for action against the mobs. In two days of fighting, the mobs had sustained tremendous losses. No one would ever count the dead or injured. Still, the issue was not resolved and if victory were measured by the mobs' disruption of orderly city life they had won their war. At least, they thought they had. Saloons stayed open all night in the lower wards. And there was high revel. Commissioner Kennedy would not bother them for awhile. Colonel O'Brien would never again order his troops to open fire.

But actually they had already lost. At midnight that night the news came to Mayor Opdyke's emergency headquarters at the St. Nicholas Hotel. It was from Secretary of War Edwin M. Stanton. Five regiments had been detached from the regular Army and assigned to put down the insurrection in New York City . . .

Wednesday, July 15th. It dawned hot. It would be the hottest day of the year. The excitement had spread to Brooklyn where grain elevators were set afire. Thousands of people had fled the city. Streets usually crowded were deserted now. No Negro dared leave his home. Many were hidden in homes uptown. They huddled in cellars and were fed stealthily and in secret. Sometimes they could hear the mobs as they swaggered through the streets looking for Negroes. They sat in silence and spoke in whispers and prayed and were grateful for the darkness and for brave friends who had taken them in while the madness was on the city.

And the fighting continued. There was a special meeting of the Common Council, and the aldermen voted a bill permitting the city to borrow $2,500,000 so that any New Yorker who was called in the draft could request the city to pay the $300 needed for exemption. Later the figure was raised to $3,750,000.

Negroes were attacked and hanged on Eighth Avenue that morning and it took six rounds of artillery to disperse the mob. Evening came and the sun slanted toward the Hudson, but the heat remained. A detachment of two hundred and fifty soldiers with two howitzers attacked a mob on First Avenue, but were frustrated when the rioters sought refuge in houses along the street. The howitzers were brought into action but were ineffective against the rioters who would take cover until they were fired and then stand up to fire their weapons out of windows and from doorways. The troops slowly withdrew. This was a job for the police with their nightsticks. The mob, sensing victory, stormed out of the houses and attacked with wild fury. The troops, many of them veterans of Confederate attacks, stood their ground for a moment, then broke and fled ignominiously down the street. Their commanding officer, a colonel, was wounded. With a bullet in the thigh, he took refuge in a house but was soon discovered. Two of his companions were clubbed to death, but one of the rioters who had known and liked the colonel managed to save him. Hours later, a woman who lived in the house located a surgeon, and he survived.

It was another victory for the mob. For three days now, they had owned the city. Maybe the time would come when there would be no more police to oppose them. No more soldiers. There were rumors of the riots spreading to Newark. Riots, too, in Boston. A group of Confederate prisoners was scheduled to arrive that day in Jersey City. They were re-routed. Two men on horseback ride up to a mob at Third Avenue and Thirty-third Street and ask for three cheers for Jeff Davis. It is given. And a reporter mentions the brief appearance of the mysterious Mr. Andrews of Virginia who extorted the mobs on that first day across from the recruiting office. He seems to be in a position of leadership now. He is mounted on a horse. And he has a saber. And he wants the fighting to go on.

And it does. There will be fighting for two more days. At

ten o'clock Wednesday night, the Fourth Regiment of the National Guard entered the city and was marched through the ominous streets where the rioters could watch. A half an hour later, the Sixty-fifth Regiment arrived and it, too, was sent on parade through the lower city. All night there was heat down there and the sound of marching feet. At four o'clock in the morning, the Seventh Regiment, no stranger to mobs, landed at Canal Street. Early morning found them, too, moving in disciplined files through the streets. Later in the morning, the Sixty-ninth Regiment arrived. Then the Twenty-sixth Michigan and the Fifty-second and Hundred and Fifty-second New York Volunteers. And there were more. All day troops were arriving in the city. And all the next day. Battle-hardened troops. Men who had faced the enemy in the South and were ready to face this enemy too.

Fighting continued throughout Thursday and, to a less extent, on Friday. But the riot was really over. The troops ended it. Their presence gave the police a chance to rest and nurse their wounds. The city was divided into four districts. And the streets were patrolled constantly and in force. Mobs were broken up before they had a chance to form. Transportation started again. Rails were repaired and telegraph wires restrung. It was over.

And there was time then for a summing up. The casualties of the fighting were estimates; there were no precise statistics kept by those who dragged their dead away to nameless graves in the Five Points cellars or the East River. Conservative estimates put the number killed at over two thousand—roughly the number of American battle casualties in the War of 1812. There were at least eight thousand wounded. Practically every member of the Police Department was injured but, incredibly, only three died. The War Department did not release figures of the military who were killed but it was at least fifty, with some three hundred wounded. Eighteen

Negroes were hanged and seventeen were reported missing.

Police and military captured some eleven thousand pistols and muskets along with some seven thousand bludgeons. More than a hundred buildings were burned and two hundred others looted and damaged. Property loss was about five million dollars, not including the hundreds of thousands of dollars lost because of the stoppage of business. It has been estimated that some fifty-to-seventy thousand men and women took part in the rioting, with individual mobs swelling on occasion to ten thousand.

But of all these, only nineteen persons were tried and convicted. They were sentenced to an average of five years each in prison.

The smoke from the fires had not yet blown away before the questions began to be asked. Why had it happened? Who was to blame? Many thought of it as a Catholic insurrection. They pointed out that while scores of buildings were burned, no Catholic property was damaged. A Methodist Episcopal Mission in the Five Points had been looted and burned by a mob that shouted the praises of the Pope. And some carried banners reading DOWN WITH PROTESTANTISM. Early in the rioting, the Mayor and the Governor had requested Archbishop John Hughes, the highest ranking Catholic prelate in the city, to address the rioters and demand a halt. This he refused to do until the military had taken control and the riot ended. And even then his words were consoling rather than disciplinary.

On Thursday posters had appeared throughout the city. Each was an invitation to the men of New York, "who are called in many of the papers rioters," to come to and hear him speak. "Men," it read, "I am not able, owing to the rheumatism in my limbs to visit you, but that is not a reason why you should not pay me a visit in your whole strength. Come, then, tomorrow. Friday at 2 o'clock to my residence, northwest corner of Madison Avenue and Thirty-sixth Street. I shall have a speech prepared for you."

They were there. They were there by the thousands. But not the rioters. News reporters noted that there were no bandages, no black eyes, no swollen heads. The Archbishop sat in a chair on his balcony. There was quiet and he spoke.

"Every man has a right to defend his home or his shanty at the risk of life. The cause, however, must be just. It must not be aggressive or offensive. Do you want my advice? Well, I have been hurt by the report that you were rioters. You cannot imagine that I could hear these things without being grievously pained. Is there not some way by which you can stop these proceedings and support the laws, none of which have been enacted against you as Irishmen and Catholics? You have suffered already. No government can save itself unless it protects its citizens. Military force will be let loose upon you. The innocent will be shot down and the guilty will be likely to escape. Would it not be better to retire quietly?"

It was a good speech. But it came too late. This was Friday. The arrival of the military had made his talk academic.

But it was neither a Catholic insurrection nor a Catholic plot. The rioters being mostly Irish immigrants were, of course, Catholic. But they were not bent on Catholic errands, although they were themselves sometimes confused and so some of the violence was done in the name of protection against heretics. But most of the police were Irish, too, and Catholic, and no police have ever worked harder or stood more resolute in the face of danger or showed more courage or devotion to duty than the police during those first three terrible days. The riots had been born of hatred for an unjust draft law. But their beginnings had been nurtured long and were non-Catholic in origin. These people had been taught resentment. Wood, a renegade Quaker, had taught them that.

Tweed, too, was their teacher, and Isaiah Rynders who believed only in the ritual of self-interest and the sacrament of violence.

Mayor Opdyke would not survive in politics, and never again would he ever covet official life. Governor Seymour would remember those days. Later, when he was a candidate for the Presidency of the United States, his opponents would summon back the memory. If he cannot control a mob, they would say, how can he preside over a nation. And he lost the election.

Rynders was an old man and already half-forgotten when the draft riots began. One imagines him walking the streets in those terrible days, listening to the voices and reaping the whirlwind. Did he regret his past? Did he remember his own words artfully contrived to plead seemingly for peace while actually calling for violence? *Workmen, shall Americans or Englishmen rule in this city? . . . We advocate no violence but a free expression of opinion to all public men. Washington forever! Stand by your lawful rights!* He was old now and he walked the streets and looked into their faces and they were the children of his children. *Blanks! Their guns are loaded with blanks.* Thirty-seven had died that day. And it was all just rehearsal for this.

There was a brief and almost plaintive postscript to the riots in the *New York Tribune* of Friday, July 17, 1863, the last day of the turmoil: "Ex-U.S. Marshall Rynders applied to General Stafford yesterday for a sufficient number of arms to protect his house against the violence of the rioters."

The request was denied.

CHAPTER 7

"THERE IS A TIDE IN THE AFFAIRS OF MEN . . . "

> "Talk about corruption of the past! Talk about the robbing of the City Treasury in the past! My God, when these tremendous powers are vested in this mayor, and when his appointments are made under these powers that you are now giving him what has been done in that way in the past will be nothing to what will be done in the future!"
> — New York State Senator Thomas J. Creamer.

ON THE MORNING OF MAY 5, 1870, probably between the hours of ten and noon, William Marcy Tweed stole five and a half million dollars.

It was city money and it was easy. Tweed was a member of the newly formed Board of Audit which replaced the old Board of Supervisors. It was an appropriation for the county courthouse and out of an authorization of $6,312,500 dollars, nearly ninety percent was split up among the members of the now well-established "Ring."

It was a Thursday. The newspapers make no mention of the incident. But it is duly reported that day that six Negroes found playing draw poker for pennies in the basement of 208 West Thirtieth Street had been arrested and were being held for trial.

149

Tweed had other sources of revenue. He owned the *Daily Transcript* which had become the official newspaper of the City of New York. As such, it received huge amounts of city advertising at splendid rates. Tweed also was part owner of the New York Printing Company which did all the city printing. He was also the proprietor of the Manufacturing Stationer's Company which supplied the city with stationery. One bill indicates the profits he made on this arrangement. One of the city departments ordered from Tweed's company a modest number of supplies which were duly delivered. These were six reams of foolscap paper—about three thousand sheets. There were six reams of note paper, two dozen penholders, four inkbottles, a dozen sponges and three dozen boxes of rubber bands. The bill for this was $10,000.

Tweed was living well. He had moved to a fine mansion and delighted in writing the address, number 511 Fifth Avenue. It was on the southeast corner of Fifth and Forty-third Street. He had nice neighbors and fountains in the front yard. He sent his children to private schools and bought a yacht. His solution of the mooring problem was characteristic. He founded his own yacht club. A group of old fire cronies had organized informally for periodic swimming and fishing trips to Connecticut. And, sentimentally, they called their group the "Americus Club." Tweed took over this group, built a large clubhouse on the beach front at Greenwich and raised the initiation fee to one thousand dollars. Membership was indicated by the acquisition of a gold pin contrived in the shape of a tiger's head. The eyes were made of rubies. A pin cost two thousand dollars.

Tweed also acquired a mistress. She was blonde and short enough to walk under Tweed's outstretched arms. She probably had other accomplishments equally interesting, but Tweed's influence inhibited discussion of this and very little survives to form a picture. Tweed secreted her away in a big house near his Connecticut club and there, for the most part, she stayed, remote, mysterious, well supplied with the necessaries of life, and probably bored to tears.

Tweed was supposed to be worth $12,000,000. He would later say this was wrong, that he was never worth more than $3,000,000. But by then he was having to account for the sources of his wealth. In 1870 he was beholden to no one. The diamond he wore on the front of his shirt was the size of a small cherry. He dined mostly at the Astor House and Delmonico's. And he always paid the check, no matter who had suggested the dinner. He was garrulous in the presence of small social groups but had a curious reticence before crowds. He spoke rapidly, sometimes to the point of incoherence, and he seemed to have a genuine fear of being called upon to make a formal speech. Others would speak for him almost always. There would be cheers for the Boss. But he said little in public. It was almost as though he recognized that he was, above all, a conspirator and that his most important pronouncements would always be spoken in a whisper.

Still he dreamed of magnificence and walked as though he were wearing a toga. The *New York Herald* reported that Tweed had offered a Roman Catholic priest a half million dollars to develop some kind of a charitable institution on the site of his birthplace at Number One Cherry Street. Tweed would have liked that. The generations that followed would have passed this place and read that here a great man was born.

It was not to be, however. The area was scheduled to be demolished to make way for the approaches of the Brooklyn Bridge. And the Tweed birthplace is lost now under the abutments. The bridge is a much better memorial to Tweed than anything he could have invented. The sponsors of the Bridge found that in order to get approval for the issuance of the bonds, some $65,000 would have to be passed out among the honorable city councilmen. Tweed was asked to handle the arrangements and did. There were also other arrangements. Tweed was given a block of stock with a par value of $40,000 in the Bridge Company and later he became a director of the corporation. And Number One Cherry Street disappeared in a disorderly confusion of steel and cement and corruption . . .

In 1867, Tweed decided to enlarge his field of activity. New York City was his almost as if he had staked it out and taken squatter's rights. But all his powers ended at the city line. As in the past, the state legislature remained the great restraining factor. The unlamented Mayor Wood had met this enemy and been defeated. Tweed would not make the mistakes of his teacher. He decided not to oppose the legislature, but to join it.

So he ran for state senator. He might have been excused from assuming more responsibilities. He was already school commissioner of the City of New York. He was assistant street commissioner, president of the Board of Supervisors of the County of New York, and chairman of the Democratic Central Committee of the county. His family saw him only briefly now and at rare intervals. Even his mistress was feeling a little ignored.

It wasn't much of a campaign and would have been completely routine had not Fernando Wood returned to haunt the election. Wood revived the old Mozart Hall Democracy that year and ran for mayor against Hoffman, the regular Tammany candidate. Wood made a surprisingly good showing, gathering in 22,930 votes and beating the Republican candidate. But Hoffman carried the field easily with 63,030 votes.

Wood, that year, also entered a candidate for state senator in opposition to Tweed. The man's name was Bagley. Tweed received 15,446 votes; Bagley, by official count, got 9. Wood never challenged Tweed again.

Tweed was forty-five now, gross, amiable, profane and enormously successful. Mayor Hoffman frankly owed his position to Tweed and would soon be made governor. Tweed was literally surrounded by friends or, at least, confederates. The elegant A. Oakey Hall was his district attorney and Tweed owned at least two judges of the state supreme court, Albert Cardozo and George G. Barnard. Judge Barnard was, to use a kind word, eccentric. He had graduated from Yale College and set out for California where, so went the rumor, he had been occasionally employed as a stool pigeon in a gambling house. He retired from this activity for a brief career as a performer with a Negro minstrel troupe.

But feeling that his talents were not being fully utilized, he returned to New York City, entered Tammany politics, became a friend of Tweed, and, in 1858, city recorder. Tweed later made him justice of the New York supreme court. It was pleasant work and Judge Barnard chose to ignore a remark made by his brother that "George knows as much law as a yellow dog." He usually whittled small pine sticks while cases were being argued before him and there was always a pile of scrapings on the floor beside his bench. His comments on the bench were highly irregular. Later, when charges were brought against him by the Bar Association, a witness testified that once, in a case involving alleged adultery by a wife, her attorney told the court that the charge was false and that the defendent was in court to prove it. "What of that?" Judge Barnard answered. "Do you think I can tell whether she has committed adultery by looking at her?" The witness later pointed out that the words he had quoted were not precisely those of the judge, who, presumably, had used a more stark expression.

Judge Cardozo was rather more restrained in appearance

and action. But he was available to carry out Tweed's orders
and his apparent mildness was deceiving. One description
of Cardozo survives: "He had the eyes of a serpent looking
out from the face of a corpse." The disgrace he brought to
his name would be lifted a generation later by the dignity,
wisdom and integrity of a son, Benjamin Nathan Cardozo
who would serve long and well as an Associate Justice of the
United States Supreme Court.

Judge John H. McCunn of the Superior Court was another Tweed protégé who had attracted the favorable attention of the Boss when, during the Draft Riots, he had
discharged a prisoner on the grounds that the Draft Act was
unconstitutional, void and inoperative.

Richard Connolly, practical and avaricious and loyal—at
least so long as it served his purpose to be loyal, was comptroller, and Peter B. Sweeny, scheming and withdrawn, was
city chamberlain. In 1869 Hoffman became governor, according to Tweed's plans, and "Elegant" Oakey Hall was
promoted to the mayor's chair.

At the top of the pyramid, of course, was Tweed himself,
grand sachem and state senator. And he had a precisely
defined chain of command. Sweeny was in charge of the
judiciary and selected candidates for the bench. Connolly
was the financial expert of the group and brought to their
involved affairs the splendid organization that could only
have come from one experienced in banking. Hall had been
a brilliant lawyer and was in charge of making certain that
their activities stayed as closely as possible within the letter
of the law.

This was the Tweed Ring. Governor Hoffman was not
properly a member. He did not benefit from their stealing.
He was simply always ready to carry out their orders in
silence and in gratitude.

By January 1, 1869, the Ring virtually controlled the city.

There is one story, not completely documented, which illustrates the general tenor of the times. Candidates for admission to the Bar were compelled to appear for examination before a judge of the state supreme court. A contemporary writer reported that this question-and-answer passage took place before Judge Barnard:

"Now, sir, if you had a claim for a client of $50,000 against the City, what would be the first step you would take to recover it?"

"I would go and see Bill Tweed."

"You will make your mark as a corporation lawyer."

Tweed had moved far from the little furniture shop on Cherry Street and the very memory must have seemed like that of another life in another world. Shortly before Christmas of 1870, there was a collection for the poor of the Seventh Ward. Tweed put himself down for a gift of $5,000. "Oh, Boss," said the solicitor, "put another zero to it!" Tweed didn't hesitate but casually raised his gift to $50,000.

It was a period of money flamboyance. Jim Fisk and Jay Gould and Vanderbilt and the others were dealing in millions daily and for some of them money ceased to have significance or reality. One of the carpets for the Americus Club had been manufactured in England at a cost of $3,600. One of the members described it proudly. It was, he said, as thick as a beefsteak.

Under Tweed, the city treasury was made an adjunct to Tammany charities; precise records were kept. Between 1869 and 1871, the city contributed $1,396,388.51 to the Catholic church for its schools and charities, and other denominations came in for ample—if less dramatic—sums. The Protestant Episcopal church received $56,956.72. Synagogues were next, with gifts adding up to $25,851.56. Presbyterian churches received $13,960.52; the Methodist Episcopal church got $7,270.95, and the Baptists were at the bottom of

the list with $5,325.63. It is not a matter of record whether
the Baptists were richer than most and hence did not need
city charity, or had perhaps shocked the Ring by their
refusal to renounce the world, the flesh and the Republican
party.

By 1869, Tweed looked like a senator. He looked like a
Roman senator, fat and secure and conspiring. He took up
quarters in the Delevan House in Albany and, in a short
time, members of the state legislature, never an inspiring
group, were conducting themselves like the old aldermanic
Forty Thieves. They were afraid of Tweed from the beginning. He arrived in Albany as the acknowledged head of the
Democratic organization in New York City and he had a lot
of money to play around with. Normally, as head of the city
machine, he would have played a secondary role to the state
party chairman, Samuel Jones Tilden. But Tweed felt uncomfortable playing a subservient part to anyone. And he
thoroughly detested Tilden who was ambitious, articulate,
well liked and cautiously honest. And it was part of the
nature of Tweed that, having decided Tilden was not his
friend, he regarded him as his enemy.

Tweed set about consolidating his power. His suite in the
Delevan House was a conversation piece. There were seven
rooms. Six of them were reception and conference rooms,
the seventh was a bedroom for the Boss. The suite was
expensively furnished and showed what could be done with
care, patience, money, and unlimited bad taste. There was
an excess of potted plants and cut flowers, and near each
window there were brass cages—each with a canary bird.
There were sideboards in each room laden with a profusion
of cut glass, whiskey and gin. Steel engravings hung on the
wall, and in one room there was—for some reason never made
quite clear—a square grand piano. The porcelain cuspidors
were daintily rimmed with painted decorations representing

sprays of roses. All of this was for the entertainment of the guests. Tweed did not smoke and, while at one time a fairly heavy drinker, now confined his drinking to an occasional sip of wine.

He really didn't have time for extracurricular sin. He was a single purposed man who put in a long day manipulating public funds. And his day was apt to begin early. Normally people who wanted preferential treatment in the legislature would go to the speaker of the assembly. Tweed's arrival ended that. They came now to the Delevan House. Hoffman came, of course. A. Oakey Hall, Connolly and Sweeny came, too, and there were more. When Jay Gould and Jim Fisk, Jr., were engaged in their outrageous campaign to win the Erie railroad from Commodore Vanderbilt, they often visited Delevan House. Tweed, first an ally of the old Commodore, changed allegiance and instructed Judge Barnard to accommodate his new-found friends in any decisions that might have to be handed down. Gould and Fisk were very pleased with the arrangement. And they were delighted to pay for the special privileges that Tweed and Sweeny provided for them. Sweeny, apparently, was particularly helpful. In a three-year period he received $150,000 for his services to Erie. In the same period Tweed was handed $105,000. In both cases the sums went into the books as "legal expenses."

Tweed organized the state legislature as he had organized the old Forty Thieves. Prior to Tweed's arrival on the scene, the legislators had been corrupt and disorganized. Tweed exulted in their corruption but deplored their disunity and lack of organization. In effect, he put them on a paying basis and converted their haphazard peculations into a system.

There were objections, of course. And honest men. Or one, at least. His name was E. M. K. Glenn and he represented the Second District of Wayne County. When the Erie fight was going on, he rose on the floor of the Assembly and charged that some of the members of that august house were receiving bribes. One can imagine the stony silence that must have followed his remarks. He had himself, he said, been offered $500. And he demanded that a committee of investigation be appointed by the speaker. The speaker, Tweed's man to the fingertips, readily complied with the request.

A committee was duly appointed and dispatched on its errands. The members presented themselves at the Erie offices and demanded to see the books. The request was granted and the books produced. To the participants, the whole incident must have seemed like some ritualistic pantomime at which no one was allowed to laugh. After an examination of the books, the members returned to the assembly where they solemnly reported that the Honorable Member from Wayne County must have been misinformed. The books showed that not even one penny had been appropriated to influence the legislature.

Glenn resigned in disgust and went home.

The incident might have given Tweed pause, but apparently it did not. This Glenn was just another Sturtevant. He was like Tweed's own father. And he would probably die poor.

They called the assembly members Tweed's Black Horse Cavalry. It was a good name. They were well-trained and well-disciplined. And they followed Tweed's orders without question. He had proved to them that it was profitable to do so. They voted the way he wanted and took their money and asked no questions. And Tweed held forth at the Delevan House, and his disciples came and paid tribute and listened in awe to his pronouncements. He was like some grotesque messiah come to lead the world to perfect corruption.

There were Republican newspapers in Albany, of course, and at first they were troublesome. Tweed paid off. And he was subtle. The attacks on him didn't end. They simply became ineffective. Some of the anti-Tweed articles were actually written by the Ring members themselves. They were so worded that a ringing denial could be made the next day—with proof. The editor of the *Albany Evening Journal,* a Republican paper, used to visit Tweed occasionally at his rooms. Together they would write up the political articles for the next day's editions.

It cost a lot. A thousand dollars sometimes, Tweed said later. Sometimes five thousand.

It was hard-earned money for the editor. The *Evening Journal* had been a Republican paper for years. The early articles attacking Tweed had been splendid. One thousand—five thousand . . .

The editor died shortly after his arrangements with Tweed.

The *Albany Argus* was another. At first they had been magnificently independent. But that stopped. The *Argus* was part of a company that also did printing in Albany. In 1869 Tweed ordered $176,600 worth of printing from this company. The next year it was over $270,000. And the attacks stopped.

Tweed never killed his enemies. He preferred emasculation. The New York County Republican Committee did not pass out of existence. But Tweed had fifty-nine of its leaders on his payroll.

But the opposition to Tweed, weak and disorganized, never died out altogether. The *New York Sun* went as far as it dared. Horace Greeley disliked the Ring and so expressed himself in the *Tribune.* But he was ambitious for public office and was never quite willing to have the battle lines drawn.

And opposition to Tweed took curious shapes and expressed itself in strange ways.

There was, walking the streets of New York in those years,

a truly remarkable person named George Francis Train. He had started his career in his uncle's shipping house and by the time he was twenty-two was earning $10,000 a year. He built his own fleet of ships then and two years later his income had risen to $94,000. Somewhere along the line, he was taken with the conviction that one day he would be President of the United States. Going into the always promising railroad business, he organized the peculiar-smelling "Credit Moblier" which provided gifts of railroad stock for congressmen who voted favorably. The scandal drove Train from business, but he was still quite active in his presidential campaign.

Everyone laughed at this, of course. And they laughed, too, when he would announce at street meetings that Boss Tweed was a crook. Train proposed stringent measures to correct the situation. "All in favor of Hanging Tweed say 'Aye,' " he would shout. The "ayes" were always loud and long. Tweed was amused. And Train was left undisturbed to find his destiny. He ran independently for the presidency, lost and took up the fight of Ireland against Britain and finally, white-haired and old, haunted Madison Square Park where he consistently refused to shake hands for fear, he said, of losing his psychic force. And he carried an umbrella to ward off malign influences.

Tweed was not worried about Train. But he was annoyed and bothered by Tilden. He didn't understand Tilden and his honesty. And he didn't own him. But he frightened him. Tilden early had ambitions for the White House and he simply did not dare cross Tweed and his powerful machine. If you're going to win a presidential election, it is almost imperative to carry New York State. And for a Democrat to carry New York State, he must roll up powerful majorities in New York City. So Tilden did not want to be known as an enemy of Tweed. But he disliked him intensely, and the feeling was mutual.

Everyone was watching Tweed and wondering where his adventures would lead. Tweed knew this and exulted in it. They were all afraid of him and he knew that, too. Scare them to death or, if that fails, buy them. It was as easy as that.

In the election of 1868, even New Yorkers were shocked at Tweed. Tweed wanted Hoffman elected governor. But there was every indication of a huge Republican vote upstate. He'd have to offset that. Repeaters at the polls would help, of course. But that might not be enough. Wood used to naturalize a few hundred immigrants right before election to help swell the grand total.

It was characteristic of Tweed that, having decided to use this idea of Wood's, he would improve on it. A few hundred voters wouldn't help much. But a few thousand would. Tweed set his pet judges to work. In twenty days there were sixty thousand more eligible voters in New York City. The previous average had been six thousand naturalizations a year. Judge Barnard especially rose to the occasion, giving citizenship to thirty-seven thousand immigrants.

And, of course, Hoffman won election to the governorship.

The rumblings were growing louder now. They were still faint. But they were there.

The annual assessment for taxes in New York City—less than ten million dollars in 1860—had risen to over twenty-three million in 1870. But during that time, the valuation for taxation had barely doubled. The city debt before the war was nineteen million. By the end of 1870, it had risen to seventy-three million. In 1860 the annual tax levy averaged only $4.33 cents per individual. By 1870, it was up to $25.11.

Business and professional men, editors, teachers—those who were not directly involved in the city government— were growing restive. Old Peter Cooper, who had helped dispel the Forty Thieves two decades before, roused himself again. Cooper was the head of a non-partisan organization called the Citizens' Association. It had been formed to act as a watchdog over municipal affairs. It had a membership of prominent and honorable men. The secretary of the Association was a Republican named Nathaniel Sands, and the others relied on him to keep them advised about municipal skullduggery.

Tweed approached Sands and inquired if he would be interested in a city job. Sands would. He was made tax commissioner, a job that paid $15,000 a year. What about Tweed and the Ring? Sands solemnly advised the members of the Citizens' Association that the members of the so-called Ring were all wealthy men, no longer interested in wealth, and really on the side of the taxpayers . . .

Tweed had one worry. If, in some flurry of reform, the office of city comptroller was ever taken from his control, there would be trouble. As it was, no one saw the books except the Ring members and James Watson, the very close-mouthed city auditor. But the office of comptroller was an elective one and while the Ring controlled Tammany and hence the nominations and while they could elect anyone they wanted in New York City, the possibility of error was there. Suppose—just suppose an honest man were elected comptroller and fell heir to those books. Seventy-five hundred dollars for thermometers for the County Courthouse! And for safes—$404,347.72! Tweed knew he had to arrange things so that no enemy would ever hold the comptroller's job.

His first move was ingenious—a rider attached to the tax levy bill of 1870. This provided for taking the office of comptroller from the elective list and making it an appointive job under the office of the mayor. The first appointee, furthermore, was to hold his position until January 1, 1875. The bill passed and Mayor A. Oakey Hall immediately re-appointed "Slippery Dick" Connolly. And the Ring members could breathe freely, at least for five years.

It took time to arrange all this, of course—time spent away from New York City. Tweed would dash into town occasionally. But mostly he was away. And to be away from Tammany Hall meant to lose control.

That happened to Tweed. And even as he was going from victory to victory in Albany, an opposition group developed practically on his own doorstep—in Tammany Hall itself.

They called themselves the Young Democracy, and by winter of 1870 they were well organized. They were experienced and professional, and they were out to get Tweed. It was time, they said, in the always self-conscious idiom of Tammany, for the young braves to have their own seats around the council fires. What they meant was that they wanted in on the loot.

One of the guiding lights behind the group was State Senator Thomas J. Creamer who was very popular with the German voters of the city. Another leader was Sheriff James O'Brien, a Tweed appointee who had fallen out with the Boss when the Ring refused to approve certain of his claims against the city. Tweed was usually quite open-handed when it came to handing out city money, but Sheriff O'Brien's claim was in the neighborhood of a third of a million dollars and was a little too much, even for Tweed. And he said no. O'Brien sulked for awhile, then began talking "reform." Other prominent men joined him. There was State Senator Henry W. Genet, and John Morrissey, one-time prize fighter and gambler whom Tweed had elected to the House of Representatives.

The new group had a strong appeal for the German voters because of the popularity of Creamer, and they added to this a huge number of Irish voters by announcing that an Irishman should be elected mayor.

It is highly probable that Tilden was advising this group. If they managed to depose Tweed, Tilden would have a clear track for the presidential nomination.

They announced their fight with Tweed in a fairly dramatic way. They submitted to the legislature a new charter for New York City.

But now Tweed went to work, too. And Sweeny helped. Together they wrote their own charter and, as their competition grew, they began to realize that their success, perhaps even their existence, depended on its passage.

The Tweed charter, as written, was an involved document so full of long and legalistic passages that its real import was difficult for contemporaries to see. But it was clear enough to Tweed. And to Sweeny and the others. It would guarantee them control of the city for as long as they were able to elect a mayor.

By their charter the mayor was given the responsibility of appointing every important official in the hierarchy of the city. First he would appoint the comptroller who, in turn, would appoint the court officials. Each department head would report directly to the mayor and only to the mayor, and no one else would know the condition of the city's affairs. These appointments were for periods of four to eight years. Furthermore, there would be established a Board of Audit which would be responsible for auditing all bills against the city. The Board was to consist of the mayor, the comptroller and the commissioner of public works. And it was understood that Tweed would be appointed to this last position. Sweeny, while not a member of the Board of Audit, would be made commissioner of public parks. The appointive power of the mayor was to be conferred only on the incumbent—for which read "Elegant" Oakey Hall—and in the case of his removal by death, disability or resignation, the same powers were to be exercised by the comptroller who, of course, was Richard B. Connolly.

New Yorkers generally approved of the Tweed charter. It seemed to provide for genuine "home rule," a subject that had been a touchy one ever since the legislature had taken the police force away from Mayor Wood, and even before.

Greeley was fooled. Senator Creamer of the Young Democracy was not. And he spoke out on the Senate floor:

"Talk about the corruption of the past! Talk about the robbery of the city treasury in the past! My God, when these tremendous powers are vested in this mayor, and when his appointments are made under these powers that you are now giving him what has been done in that way in the past will be nothing to what will be done in the future!"

Tweed let him talk. He had the votes to pass the measure. Or, at least, he had the money.

The measure was submitted to vote in the Assembly first. It was March 28, 1870, a Monday. The time had come to end the talk and be counted.

Tweed got a shock. The Young Democracy group back at Tammany Hall had called a meeting of the General Committee for that night. Tweed, as grand sachem, would have to summon the meeting. And he would have to be present. The meeting had been voted by more than half of the membership of the committee, and to refuse would be to invite his own removal. But he knew also the purpose of the meeting—a vote of non-confidence and the election of someone else as chairman of the General Committee.

Tweed left Albany, returned to New York and called a meeting as demanded. March 28th. It had been a stormy Sunday and the city streets were still cluttered with the debris from a hurricane that had beaten down over the city. Ships had been tossed around in the bay. Some houses in Brooklyn had been blown over.

By Monday the storm had cleared but the skies were lowering still and there was a threat of more rain.

Tweed had been maneuvered into a tight corner. He would have greatly preferred to have been in Albany where his new charter was scheduled to be voted on in the Assembly.

He was in New York, and it was a Young Democracy victory. He had to be there. O'Brien, Genet, Morrissey, Creamer and the others were taking on the "champ" and making it hurt. They were winning. Tweed was compelled to call the meeting for that night. They had him now. From here on in the gravy would be theirs . . .

All that day Tweed sat in his office on Duane Street. A reporter for the *Tribune* managed to squeeze through the swarm of frightened and excited politicians who jammed the stairways, and to get into Tweed's inner office. The Boss, he wrote that night, was "calm, collected and cool." But he had said little beyond the fact that he was confident of success. He added that he had offered to bet both O'Brien and Morrissey any sum from $1,000 to $25,000 that within thirty days they would be outside of the Tammany Committee. It sounded like bravado and the reporter seemed a little miffed that he was unable to take the bet himself.

Sunset and lowering clouds appeared over Fourteenth Street that night. The Young Democrats and their followers arrived early. The meeting was set for eight that night. They would have a brief pep meeting earlier in Irving Hall just around the corner. They filed into this meeting hall and noisily took their seats.

Some were strangely ill at ease about the coming events. They were, after all, taking on the Boss himself. And they had noticed that Fourteenth Street had been filled with police. Hundreds of them. No one quite knew why.

They soon found out. The Tammany sachems—Tweed's boys every one . . . had appealed to the police to close

Tammany Hall for the night. The meeting scheduled for that night, they informed the police, gave every indication of developing into a riot. Innocent people would be hurt. There would be bloodshed.

By dark there were almost more police on Fourteenth Street in front of Tammany Hall than there were civilians. There were over six hundred police mustered altogether.

Quickly the news spread among the anti-Tweed men in Irving Hall. The police have closed Tammany. No meeting tonight. You could feel the anger in the crowd. Senator Creamer was acting as chairman.

A voice from the crowd:

"Mr. Chairman, are we to understand that Police Superintendent Kennedy is the Grand Sachem of Tammany now?"

The speaker was angry. And no one laughed. And no one answered.

Senator Genet got to his feet:

"Mr. Chairman, as it is now eight o'clock and it is time that the doors of Tammany Hall be open, I move that we organize commencing with the first ward and move two by two to Tammany Hall and demand admission."

There were cheers at this. And it was done.

They didn't get in. They argued. They implored. They threatened. But they didn't get in. Bryant's Minstrel Hall next door to Tammany Hall had also been closed to give a look of authenticity to the sachems' report that the innocent must be protected. SHOO FLY, DON'T BODDER ME, the big posters read on the front of the darkened theater. Admission: fifty cents. It was almost as if the theater was in on the joke.

Senator Creamer, angry and flushed, made his way up to Inspector Walling who was in charge of the police. By whose authority is this building closed? Walling answered that it had been done by the authority of the Tammany sachems. There were other angry questions but the answer was always the same. The sachems, sir, in order to avoid a riot.

SHOO FLY, DON'T BODDER ME.

For a moment, Creamer and the others were taken back by the sheer affrontry of it. To close the hall to prevent an honest vote! It was a time to end this tyranny once and for all. What might they have done? A mass meeting in Union Square, perhaps? It was right around the corner. Their voices would have been heard. Most of the newspapers were with them. Let a meeting begin at that moment and no tyrant in the world could have stood against their voices and their votes.

At that moment it rained. It rained hard. Torrents poured down on the city. And most everyone ran for cover. And for home.

Creamer stood in the rain, conferring with the other leaders of the rebellion. This damned rain! They would hold a meeting tomorrow.

By midnight, most of the crowd had disappeared. The police, weary and wet, stayed for a little longer and then they left, too.

The Young Democracy held their meeting the next morning. But not many people came. Not a majority. Tweed had won the time he needed. Money would do the rest.

On April 19th there was another meeting called to elect new Tammany sachems. By this time, Tweed was back in control. Of the two hundred sixty-five Tammany members who assembled that night, every single one was a Tweed supporter. His re-election as grand sachem was assured. And the other nominees for sachems, including Mayor Oakey Hall, Peter Sweeny and Richard Connolly, were certain of election. Tweed secretly passed the word that twenty-three members were to vote for the now old Young Democracy. At the last minute, Tweed thought of a delicious joke. He had Tilden's name inserted on the list of nominees with

Creamer and the others. And, as planned, Tweed and his ticket were elected: two hundred, forty-three to twenty-three. Tweed would have won that bet with O'Brien and Morrissey. But he couldn't have felt bad about it. He didn't need the money . . .

The Tweed charter passed the assembly easily. And it passed in the senate too. Tilden made some timid objections, and old Horace Greeley came up to Albany to speak against it. Tweed didn't care about Tilden and he was ready for Greeley. He knew his weaknesses. The *New York Sun* reports that the old editor was met by a group of forty Republican legislators who informed him that they were seriously thinking of nominating him for governor. This was assuming, of course, that he didn't disturb things too much. Greeley's eyes must have sparkled. Governor! He made his speech, but it was an unviolent one. A few objections—a few amendments to offer . . .

No one paid much attention and Greeley packed his luggage and went back to New York. A reporter, who was with him in the hotel room as he was preparing to leave, found himself wondering what the great editor would bring with him for an overnight stay in Albany. He peeked into Greeley's bag. It held one rolled-up nightshirt and two copies of the New York *Tribune.*

Tweed said later that it cost him $600,000 to get the charter through the legislature. It was probably closer to $1,000,000.

And it was worth every penny of it. He virtually bought the city. They hung a painting of him in City Hall. There was a Tweed rally in Tweed Plaza, a small open place where East Broadway crossed Canal Street. The Boss didn't show up, but he sent a message. Part of it was revealing:

"I congratulate you, fellow citizens, upon the restoration of municipal rights. I trust our victory will, by wise use of its fruits, result in raising our party above the plane of selfish aggrandizement and redound to the harmony and success of our majestic Metropolis and throughout the State and Union."

The Union!

And why not? Tweed ran the city. And he controlled the state. It was only natural that he should begin thinking in terms of the country. He would make Governor Hoffman President. It would be easy. The first steps had already been taken when August Belmont had been dumped as national chairman of the Democratic Party. Tilden was identified with the short-lived, now defunct, Young Democracy.

Hoffman President! And Tweed would run the country. He would be a senator and stay in the background. But he would run things. There is some hint that he speculated about becoming Ambassador to the Court of St. James.

There was one cloud on the horizon. It was small. It was no bigger than a man's fist. But it was there.

The ousting of Belmont as national chairman had not gone unnoticed. Thomas Nast, late of the little school on Chrystie Street and now a political cartoonist on *Harper's Weekly,* had noticed the incident. And he had been disturbed over the high-handed way in which it had been maneuvered.

September 11, 1869. Nothing special about that day, it seemed. The papers carry the story of a train wreck on the Delaware division of the Erie Railway two and a half miles west of Port Jervis. Four crewmen were killed. A display of northern lights began at midnight and continued until 4 A.M. . . .

And on that day the regular edition of *Harper's Weekly* was delivered to subscribers. There was a Nast cartoon in the magazine. It showed Belmont being ousted as national Democratic chairman. And in the background but clear and unmistakable, you can make out the face and figure of William Marcy Tweed.

CHAPTER 8

"WANTED—HONEST MEN"

> "Let's stop them damned pictures. I don't care much what
> the papers write about me—my constituents can't read. But,
> damn it, they can see pictures!"
>   — William Marcy Tweed, 1870.

A LOT OF PEOPLE WERE SHOCKED by the cartoon, and there
was speculation as to what would happen to *Harper's* in
general and to Thomas Nast in particular.

Nothing happened. At first. Tweed was amused and for-
giving. What is one magazine? Especially one that is a little
high-brow and calls itself a "Journal of Civilization." It was
a mighty small voice and Tweed did nothing.

But Nast did. He drew another cartoon and it was published in time for Christmas Eve, 1869.

Warm for Christmas Eve in New York. Thirty-three degrees at nine that morning and it got up to forty degrees by
six that night. Edwin M. Stanton, Secretary of War under
Lincoln, died. Smallpox was on the increase, according to
a report from the Board of Health, and five bulls broke free
in an upper East Side street and had to be shot by policemen.
And *Harper's* came out with its Christmas edition.

This second cartoon was even more harsh than the first.
It showed the members of the Ring hovering over a large box

171

marked "Taxpayers' and Tenants' Hard Cash." They were breaking it open. It was a striking drawing, but the timing was bad. Most readers didn't bother to look at the magazine until the next day. And then it was Christmas and a time for family celebrations and visits and walking in the streets. At Trinity Church that Christmas, the carillon played "Once In David's Royal City." No one spoke much of politics or of Nast.

Still, Nast had gone far since the days when he had studied English and arithmetic in that little school down on Chrystie Street. He lived in Harlem in a neat little house, crowded with heavy Victorian furniture and a copy of the Venus de Milo. He had published a drawing in *Leslie's Weekly* at the age of fifteen and from then on his future work was clearly indicated. He had gone to Italy to sketch Garibaldi's fight for independence. He had gained some fame by a drawing of the Heenan-Sayers prize fight in 1860, and he had joined *Harper's* in time to draw a large number of faintly sentimental and naive sketches of scenes of the war.

By 1869, Nast was neither sentimental nor naive. He was tough and courageous and he hated injustice and bullies. And he remembered being frightened by a bully back in school—a kid dressed in fireman's clothes.

And he fashioned a symbol for Tweed and the Ring and, eventually, for all of Tammany. It was a tiger's face, the same tiger's face that had snarled down from Tweed's Big Six Company back in the days when Tweed was foreman and both were young and neither had heard of the other.

And the cartoons continued. They were relatively mild at first, not out of fear or compassion but simply because his talent for destruction had not yet achieved its later heights. To be good at hating takes practice. One improves slowly. And he was still fighting alone.

But that would change.

There was in the city of New York another enemy of Tweed. And, like Nast, he was a journalist. George Jones, co-founder with H. J. Raymond—of the *New York Daily Times* and now publisher, was growing restive. This conspiracy of silence about Tweed and the Ring was not to his liking. Everyone knew they were all crooks. But, except for Nast and *Harper's,* there was no one to speak out. The *Tribune* and the *Herald* pouted occasionally about the state of things. But they did nothing drastic and the situation called for drastic measures. Jones recognized that he had no actual facts to sustain any charges. He did not have access to the city's books. But he knew enough and he suspected more. And he was ready to fight.

But Tweed was a subtle opponent. And the *Times* was too important a voice in the community to be allowed to pursue an unfettered way. One of the three directors and a principal stockholder of the *Times,* one James B. Taylor, was an intimate of Tweed and a business partner with him in the New York Printing Company. This company was still dealing almost exclusively with the city and had received most of the $7,168,212.23 which the Ring appropriated for advertising and printing in one two-and-one-half year period. It is easy to see why Taylor was cold to any suggestions that a campaign be started against the Ring. Jones fretted and fumed and sent reporters out on stories about fires and cornerstones and bided his time.

On August 22, 1870, Taylor died. Jones waited almost a month and then let go.

It started in the edition of September 20, 1870. Most of the Tammany bigwigs were in Rochester, New York, at a nominating convention for the elections coming up the following month. But the convention was just a gesture. The Tweed candidates had it all wrapped up. Everyone knew it. But you didn't say so. And above all, you didn't write about it. Jones, no writer himself, consulted with his chief editorial assistant, Louis John Jennings, and they fired their first round. Not on Page One. The Franco-Prussian War was under way, and there were other matters that readers would be looking for and were interested in—Joe Jefferson playing *Rip Van Winkle* at the Booth Theater on Twenty-third Street and Sixth Avenue; Yellow fever again. In New Orleans this time.

It came out on the editorial page. Jennings was writing, with Jones looking over his shoulder: "Let the Rochester Convention construct its delusive platform as it may, it can never shake off the odium which Tweed and company have fastened upon the very name of Democracy. The whole confederation will be buried beneath the ruins of a system which is regarded with indignation and abhorrence by all men who haven't sacrificed honor for private gain."

The next day more of the same: "The Democrats who meet at Rochester today will have nothing to say against the monstrous abuses for which the great Mr. Tweed and his associates are responsible . . . What one man is so potent today in the Democracy of the state as Mr. Tweed? The rural Democracy may not like him. But Mr. Tweed cares nothing for their opinion one way or another. Can they destroy a fortune acquired with the rapidity which exceeds the wildest story in the *Arabian Nights?*"

Samuel Tilden, who would be a candidate for President when it was all over, spoke that day at Rochester. He made no mention of the *Times'* attack. He talked about Prussia, evoked the ghosts of Jefferson and Jackson, but said nothing that would annoy the Tweed faction. The time for Tilden had not yet come.

Jones and Jennings were in it up to their necks. One week later this appeared on the editorial page: "Shall we still bend the neck to the yoke of this Tweed rabble . . . or rise, as becomes free men, and shake it off?"

New Yorkers had never read anything like this. First that cartoonist on *Harper's* and now the *New York Times*. It wasn't just the occasional wrist-slapping that other papers did. This was real. And somebody was going to get hurt.

Tweed and the others came back from Rochester full of confidence in themselves, contempt for this latest "reform" wave, and with plans to re-elect Hoffman governor and Hall mayor. Obviously neither Nast nor *The Times* had any proof of wrongdoing or it would have come out. Nobody had talked, and the comptroller's books were safely locked in the office. Of course, the attacks were a little annoying. And if they proved bothersome, Nast and Jones would have to be paid off. If that didn't work, they could be frightened off. To Tweed, it was all a very old story. At this point he did not realize that he was up against something new. It was 1870 and he had won too often and too long.

The elections were in November. Republican leaders, goaded into action by Nast and Jones, spoke darkly about Tammany violence at the polls and finally decided to do something about it. They appealed to President Grant, described the voting situation in New York City and asked for help. The old General was shocked. The rules of fair play were being violated by these upstart Tammany men. He pondered for a moment and gave his orders. This was one New York City election that would be fair. He ordered several regiments of troops to New York. And he stationed a couple of warships in the Hudson River. Violence at the polls? This time Tammany would not have a sympathetic police force standing by at the voting places. They would have United States troops. If they want violence, they can have it. But they have to fight the federal government this time. The commander of the New York National Guard was told that his men must be ready if they were needed to assist the United States marshall and the regular troops. Now, let's see who wins an honest election in New York!

Tammany won. It was easy. Tweed had unofficially polled the various precincts and he knew they'd win without trouble at all. In fact, it was essential that there be no violence of any kind. This way the presence of the military would reflect on the President and the Republicans. Tweed called for a big rally at Tammany Hall. It was held on the night of October 27, 1870. Tweed was there, of course, and Jim Fisk, Jr., ponderous and pompous and promising that Erie employees would, on his instructions, vote Democratic. Tweed made one of his rare speeches: "We know and feel that although the oppressor's hand is upon our throat still we must calmly resist and show that the city of New York is a peaceful, law-abiding, and, as the world knows, a well governed city."

There was applause at that. There was a lot of applause there that night. It was always fun when somebody took on the Boss. He always knew what to do.

One thing he arranged for that night was a parade. A procession of men and boys that filed by Tammany Hall in a two-mile line. Each marcher carried a Roman candle and there were many banners. One of them read HOFFMAN FOR PRESIDENT—1872. Hoffman, reviewing the parade, stood and bowed politely as the banner went by.

Still, to the close observer, this scene, so familiar, was not quite the same. It rained, for one thing, a hard, pelting rain that beat down on the city and filled the gutters and soaked the marchers and made it seem that perhaps all the forces in the universe did not entirely approve of the goings-on.

And another thing. It was nothing, really. A joke. Some anti-Tammany men managed to join the parade and, at an appropriate time, unfurled a banner reading: WANTED—

HONEST MEN. It was pretty funny. But it wouldn't have happened the year before.

The Times reported the parade in the edition of October 28th: "The whole affair is said to have cost the Ring $75,000, but as they have a corporation fund of $1,500,000 stolen from the public treasury, which they have laid by for just such emergencies as they are called upon to encounter at this time, they will scarcely feel the loss."

The Times was calling for an examination of the city's financial records. If all is well, they said, why object to having the figures made public? It was a good argument and Tweed knew he had to answer it. Imagine if *The Times* could examine the vouchers for the city! Twelve million dollars for that courthouse behind City Hall! The payoffs and the bribes!

Tweed rose to the occasion. He appointed a committee of six of the most prominent business men of the city to "examine the books." The committee was headed by John Jacob Astor, III, hardly one to be beguiled into supporting the Ring. Or so it seemed. Actually, Astor and the other members of the committee had all invested heavily in Manhattan real estate and it was imperative that they stay in the good graces of Tammany. Their taxes, for example, could be raised dramatically. On the day before the election, they published the results of their investigation into the orderliness of the city's financing. "We have come to the conclusion and certify," they said, "that the financial affairs of the city under the charge of the Comptroller are administered in a correct and faithful manner."

Hoffman was re-elected governor. Hall made it again as mayor, and again Tammany was in complete control of the city and the state. Tweed, having been under fire and successfully repulsed an attack, found himself an even greater hero than before. And his image, in the minds of some, became confused. One New Yorker, at least, thought of himself as living in the presence of a sort of latter-day George Washington. A Democratic police judge named Edward J. Shanley proposed that a statue be contrived and set up in Tweed Plaza, a stone's throw from where he had been born on the lower East Side. The proposal caught on and contributions were solicited and made.

Tweed, at first, was responsive to the idea and gave it at least tacit support. But even in this hour of his life, he had a politician's pragmatism and he began to see that what promised to make him magnificent might, in truth, make him ridiculous. He sent a pious little note to the statue committee pointing out that statues are usually erected only after the death of the individual concerned and asked that all contributions be returned. But, having decided against the statue, he carefully scrutinized the list of the contributors and the amounts given before the money was returned. He also read with interest the excuses submitted by those who did not contribute. As one of them remarked later: "It would have cost so damned little to put one's name down for a thousand dollars."

It seemed that Tweed had thought of everything and there were no chinks in his armor, no factors not under control. And it was almost true. But he couldn't really control everything. He couldn't control the weather. It didn't seem important, of course. But it was.

Monday, January 23, 1871, was a very cold day in New York and the snow that had fallen Saturday and Sunday night froze and became almost impossible to remove from the streets. At noon that day it got up to fourteen degrees and more snow fell. The carriages and wagons struggled through the snow and left deep ruts which froze again that night. You had to ride in the tracks of those who had broken the first paths through. There was ice in the harbor and the mails were delayed.

The next day, Tuesday, the snow stopped, but the cold persisted and the roads became frozen harder than ever. The *Times* commented on the weather and, on the editorial page, again blasted the Ring. But the campaign was slowing down. There were no facts to substantiate the charges. The comptroller's books were secret. Almost wearily the *Times* kept up the fight. "The fight," Jennings wrote that Tuesday, "is between the honest section of the press, and a swindler, and the swindler will get the worst of it in the long run."

Maybe, but you could have asked good odds that they wouldn't get the worst of it. Nast and Jones were putting up a good fight. But they simply had no proof.

Tuesday night was crisp and clear. Jimmy Watson, the county auditor, and bookkeeper for the Ring, decided on a sleigh ride. Two horses were hitched up and Watson climbed in, took the reins from his driver and was off for a fast ride up Fifth Avenue.

It happened when they were coming back. The coachman had taken the reins. It was at Eighth Avenue and 130th Street. A horse, moving north in the opposite direction, broke out of his lane and dashed between the two horses pulling Watson's sleigh. The coachman was thrown aside and escaped with minor injuries. Not so Watson, he of the immaculate handwriting and well-kept ledgers. The horse in his frenzy mounted the dashboard and one heavily shod hoof crashed down on Watson's forehead.

Watson lived a week. It was a very tense week for Tweed who hurried back from Albany and stationed a twenty-four hour watch at Watson's bedside. Suppose this man should relent and make a deathbed confession! Or suppose he became delirious and began to name names and places and facts and figures!

Watson died without saying anything. The papers mentioned that he left his family well provided for . . .

Once again luck had been kind to William Marcy Tweed. He could breathe free again. The books were safe. The secrets were well kept. Now—to fill Watson's old job. Somebody equally trustworthy. He looked around. There were plenty of competent and discreet men who would like the job. It would be easy to fill. Or so he thought. Tweed was only forty-seven that winter of 1871. But he had won too long. And he had gotten soft. Winning had been too easy. And he had become just a little careless.

The county bookkeeper, Stephen C. Lyons, Jr., was advanced to Watson's old job of auditor. And an ex-newspaperman named Matthew J. O'Rourke was made bookkeeper. And around this time, James O'Brien, erstwhile sheriff and member of the Young Democracy, managed to get a city job for a young protégé, one William Copeland. Copeland was put in charge of a set of books. O'Brien had long since made amends for his momentary aberration and was presumed to be a faithful Tammany man and loyal.

No one knew then that Copeland was making copies of some of the Ring's books. And no one knew that O'Rourke was doing the same thing. While Watson was auditor, the books were never seen by anyone except Tweed and Connolly and the other members of the Ring.

But Watson was dead.

Nast continued to draw his devastating cartoons. He drew Governor Hoffman dressed as a king in ermine with Tweed standing like some distorted Falstaff at his side. Sweeny was dressed like a Vatican guard. There was a cuspidor at their feet, ugly and symbolic. Hall was shown with an ass's body. Another showed the Ring members stealing furtively from the public treasury. Their faces are clear and unmistakable.

One day at this time, Mayor Hall met Nast on the street.

Hall, always genial, said, "I have seen some of your 'hand-writing on the wall' of late."

"You shall see more of it presently," Nast answered and passed on without stopping.

Tweed mumbled something about having Nast horse-whipped, but when they passed once in Central Park, both men lifted their hats in polite greeting and said nothing.

Nast, however, was under no illusions. Threats began coming in his mail. One letter showed a drawing of him with a thread deftly tied around his neck in the fashion of a noose.

Tweed pretended unconcern. But he was vaguely disturbed in a way he had never been before. This fight was different, somehow. Privately Tweed made himself clear. "Let's stop them damned pictures," he said. "I don't care much what the papers write about me—my constituents can't read. But, damn it, they can see pictures!"

It was a mistake to talk like that. Tweed couldn't afford to be angry. He could afford only to be shrewd and smart.

The cartoons continued. Tweed made his decision: "That's the last straw. I'll show them damned publishers a new trick."

Tweed gave orders to the Board of Education to reject any bids made by the Harper publishing company to supply the city with school books. And those currently in use were thrown out. It amounted to about $50,000 worth of books. Some members of the Harper firm became frightened, and at a meeting suggested that the anti-Tweed campaign be called off. Fletcher Harper, founder of *Harper's Weekly* and co-founder of the publishing company, staunchly refused to be either frightened by Tweed or distracted from the fight. Still, as the other members pointed out, it was beginning to cost money. They held a meeting and cautioned Harper to drop the Nast cartoons. Fletcher Harper's words of that day survive: "Gentlemen, you know where I live. When you are ready to continue the fight against these scoundrels, send for me. In the meantime, I shall find a way to continue it alone."

And *Harper's Weekly* continued to publish the Nast cartoons. One showed Tweed invading a classroom and snatching a book away from a child. Connolly is seen throwing Harper's books out of the window. Mayor Hall is at the blackboard writing maxims: "Hoffman will be our next president. Hall is a friend of the poor."

Tweed had lost his temper and the fight too. He turned his attack to the *Times*. The first thing he tried to do was buy it or at least buy enough stock so that he could control the editorial policy as Taylor had done.

He went to Raymond's widow and offered her a good price for the stock her husband had left her. The deal was within a half an hour of being consummated when Jones hurried over and bought the stock by offering a higher price than Tweed.

Tweed was beginning to realize that this fight was going a little differently from all the others and he tried something else. He had city lawyers search title to the property on which the *Times* building stood and, of course, they declared that the title was faulty. It seems the property had once been owned by a church and there was a law against conducting a business on sanctified land.

Actually, the title was in perfect order and the argument got nowhere. And some newspapers, at first cold to the *Times'* crusade, now began to give it support. If to attack the administration means that you are to be destroyed, then the phrase "freedom of the Press" is meaningless. Tweed had lost a lot of friends on the newspapers. He couldn't afford to lose his temper. He couldn't afford to make mistakes. Always before it had been others who made mistakes: Sturtevant back in the days of the Forty Thieves; Mayor Wood; the leaders of the "Young Democracy" revolt. Tweed was angry

now and not thinking very well. Nast, Jones, Jennings—
damn them all!

And all the while, Copeland and O'Rourke were busy with
their books. And sometimes they worked quite late at night.
They worked alone. And each was keeping a separate set of
books. And they were enormously interesting: $41,746.83 for
awnings; a check for $33,129.89 made out to Fillipo Don-
aruma and endorsed "Phillip F. Dummey"; the Permit Bu-
reau spends $2,842.64 to collect $6.00 . . .

The members of the Ring were pleased with the new ap-
pointments that followed Watson's death. Copeland and
O'Rourke. It was obvious that they worked hard every day.
And, frequently, until late at night . . .

On May 31, 1871, Mary Amelia Tweed, daughter of Mr.
and Mrs. William Marcy Tweed of this city, was married to
Mr. Arthur Ambrose Maginnis of New Orleans. It was a
lovely wedding. An early morning rain ended by late afternoon and the weather was clear and warm by the time the
wedding party left for church. There was Tweed walking
down the aisle with Mary Amelia, past the congregation, past
the mural of Judas slinking from the Last Supper: "Thou
Shalt Love Thy God. None Other Shalt Thou Serve."

James Fisk, Jr., was at the reception, Peter Sweeny, Mr.
Comptroller Connolly, Andrew J. Garvey, a plasterer who,
the Ring books could show, once made $133,187.20 in two
days of plastering . . .

There is no record that ex-Sheriff James O'Brien was on
hand for the festivities. Earlier that very day he had resigned
from city employ. He was still angry about that bill which
the Ring had refused to pay. It was for $350,000 which,
O'Brien said, was owed to him by the county. Just what services he performed to the value of $350,000 are not clear. At
any rate the Ring refused to pay.

O'Brien took a copy of Copeland's books with him when

he left. June came and passed and he did nothing. Then, the first week in July, he appeared at the *Times'* office.

It was night and it was hot. Jennings was in the editor's chair busy with the next day's edition. No big news, really. The federal public debt had been reduced in June by over seven million dollars; a bust of Washington Irving had been unveiled in Prospect Park with appropriate ceremonies; a man named Frank Rust, who lived at 318 Second Avenue, had been held up in the entranceway to the New York Trust Company at 119 Broadway and robbed of two thousand dollars.

O'Brien remarked that it was a hot night. Jennings allowed that it was. There was a brief pause and then O'Brien said, "You and Nast have had a hard fight."

"Have still," Jennings answered.

"I said you have had it."

And then it happened. O'Brien laid the transcripts down on Jennings' desk. And it was all there. The payments for the County Courthouse—Ingersoll's cut—Garvey. Each man was named and the amounts specified . . .

O'Brien was speaking: "Here are the proofs of all your charges—exact transcriptions from Dick Connolly's books. The boys will likely murder you when they know you've got 'em, just as they've tried to murder me."

But Jennings wasn't listening. He was reading. O'Brien left and midnight came and Jennings read on, slowly turning the pages. And he was still reading when the dawn crept silently through the windows . . .

On Saturday, July 8, 1871, the *Times* published the first of the staggering statistics: ten lofts were rented as armories by the city at a total cost of $85,500. *Times'* reporters had checked the addresses. None of them actually was used by the city. The Ring had paid out $190,600 for armories in use for

which a fair rent would have been $46,600. The arrangement
was made between Tweed and his old partner in the chair
business, James H. Ingersoll. On July 20, another blast:
". . . the following sums were paid for keeping ten armories
in repair for nine months:

A. J. Garvey, for plastering	$197,330.24
John H. Geyser, for plumbing	142,329.71
J. H. Ingersoll, for chairs	170,729.60
G. S. Miller, for carpentry work	434,064.31
Total	$943,453.86"

Two days or so after O'Brien appeared with his books,
O'Rourke also came to the *Times'* office. More of the same.

Now the *Times* had all the ammunition it wanted. Let the
Ring members get out of this one. Mayor Hall tried. But it
was a pretty feeble try. The books in the possession of the
Times, he said, came from a dishonest employee. Never mind
where they came from, Jennings wrote, the point is they are
a true account and the Mayor cannot deny them . . .

He couldn't. Neither could Tweed or Connolly or Sweeny.
Tweed was the leader and they looked to him. He had been
in fights like this before. He had learned his trade back with
the old Forty Thieves. Tweed would think of something.

Tweed did think of something. But it wasn't very good. He
put out the story that Jennings had once worked for the
London Times and had been fired because of untruthful reporting. Jennings had in fact worked for the *London Times,*
but he hadn't been fired. They dug a little deeper. Jennings,
it developed, was married to an actress. That shocked some
people but it wasn't enough. Tweed turned to Nast. The cartoonist, it was pointed out, had fled to this country to escape
military service. And any man who would not fight for his
country was not worthy to . . .

Nast pointed out that he was six years old when he landed in America.

Tweed's next move was inevitable but he made it reluctantly. It's always hard to spend money and especially money dishonestly earned. He'd have to buy Jones off. Jennings would follow. The only question was—how much? The Ring members met, conferred and settled on a figure. Jones was not an easy man to bribe. It would take a lot. But every man has his price. Tweed knew that if he knew anything. Jones had his price. He was human, Tweed figured. He's no different from the rest of us. We'll buy him and he'll be ours.

Connolly was chosen as the person to make the approach. He went to a lawyer's office in the *Times'* building and Jones was sent for. Jones arrived, took one look at Connolly, turned toward the door and said, "I don't want to see this man."

"For God's sake," Connolly said, "let me say one word to you."

At this Jones paused and the two men faced each other and each was at a crisis in his life and each understood and thoroughly disliked the other. Jones waited.

Connolly made his proposition. Five million dollars to lay off. Five million dollars! One can imagine the scene. July heat filling the room. The sound of a trolley, clanging uptown maybe. Five million dollars, Mr. Jones. And all you have to do is stop these articles. Five million dollars!

Jones answered slowly. And his response was noncommittal.

"I don't think the devil will ever make a higher bid for me than that."

Connolly burst into speech. It was a torrent of words. He described how one could live on five million dollars. He told of the power money like that could bring. With five million dollars there's nothing you can't buy. Connolly was a persuasive speaker. "Why, with that sum," he said, "you could go to Europe and live like a prince."

Time for decision, Mr. Jones. Time now to answer. Five million dollars.

"Yes," Jones said, "I could live like a prince, but I would know that I was a rascal."

And Connolly left.

CHAPTER 9

OF TIME AND A FIGHT
AND A PILE OF COAL

> "Well, what are you going to do about it?"
> — William Marcy Tweed, 1871.

NAST WAS NEXT. It happened on a Sunday afternoon. A representative of the Broadway Bank where the city funds were kept made a formal call at the Nast home. There was some preliminary conversation and then the banker got down to the business of the day.

"I hear," he said to Nast, "that you have been made an offer to go abroad for art study."

"Yes," Nast answered. "But I can't go. I haven't time."

"But they will pay you for your time." And then it came. "I have reason to believe that you could get a hundred thousand dollars for the trip."

Apparently Nast was a little disappointed at the figure. He recognized the bribe and he had no intention of taking anything, but professional pride was involved.

"Do you think," Nast said, "that I could get two hundred thousand?"

"Well, possibly. I believe from what I have heard in the bank that you might get it." The banker settled back. Every man has his price. A little flattery now. A hint of threat. "You have great talent, but you need study and you need rest. Besides, this Ring business will get you into trouble. They own all the judges and jurors and can get you locked up for libel. My advice is to take the money and get away."

Nast again: "Do you think I could get five hundred thousand to make that trip?"

There was not a moment's hesitation.

"You can. You can get five hundred thousand in gold to drop this Ring business and get out of the country."

That was all Nast wanted to hear. A matter of pride.

"Well, I don't think I'll do it. I made up my mind not long ago to put some of those fellows behind the bars and I'm going to put them there."

The banker rose and reached for his hat.

"Only be careful, Mr. Nast, that you do not first put yourself in a coffin."

Nast and *The Times* had done their work well. By the time Jones had exhausted his material the city—or at least that part of it not on the Tammany payroll—was seething with sullen anger. Tweed, too, was angry. A reporter spoke to him about the Ring disclosures. Tweed made no attempt to deny them. He was in a fight now, and it was like a thousand other fights he had been in on the Bowery when he was young and tough and exulted in the feeling of his fist slamming against somebody's nose. He listened in silence to the reporter's recital of the Ring's thievery. Then he threw out his answer.

"Well, what are you going to do about it?"

The answer was duly reported in the papers. And Tweed would soon find out what they would do about it.

The first hints came on September 4, 1871. In response to newspaper advertisements, a huge crowd gathered at Cooper Union. The meeting was called for eight o'clock, but by seven the streets outside were crowded and the doors were opened. The *Times* that morning had carried a recapitulation of the Ring's private accounts. And on the editorial page there was a call to arms: ". . . there has been taken from the public treasury for 1869 to 1871—$13,443,768.39. There is only one inference to be drawn from this overwhelming evidence. The city has been robbed."

It was an angry crowd that came. They quickly filled the seats and spilled out into the halls and stairways. It was a perfect late summer evening. Seventy-two degrees at six o'clock. *Jasper,* a drama based on Dickens' *Mystery of Edwin Drood,* was presented at the Grand Opera House. It was a long-run and successful play but it drew no such crowds as came that night to Cooper Union. Thousands, who could not find space inside, milled around on the streets waiting for news of what was going on inside. A platoon of police arrived to keep order. They proved helpful. Among the crowd were a few Tammany men who had hoped to start a fight that could turn into a riot. They were quickly subdued. A *Times'* reporter circulated through the crowd and reported the angry comments he heard. And he recorded, with astonishing candor and disinterest, the comment of one bystander whom he questioned. Was he angry at the Tammany disclosures? Not particularly. You see, he was hard of hearing and never tried to listen to speeches. He had come, he said, simply to see the crowds and excitement.

Promptly at eight o'clock the meeting began. Former Mayor William F. Havemeyer was by acclamation elected president of the meeting. He stepped forward and spoke. His speech was exactly what the audience had come to hear:

"Wealth, wrung in the shape of taxes from honest toil, flaunts itself in the public gaze in gorgeous array . . . in splendid equipages and in palatial residences to attest, I suppose, the provident, unadulterated, uncorruptible and radical democracy of its possessors. To eradicate these evils will require the use of the cautery and the knife in the hands of bold, skillful and faithful operators. This city, fellow citizens, now calls her people to their duty in this time of her humiliation."

There were great cheers at that. At each mention of the name of Tweed, Hall, Connolly or Sweeny, the crowd hissed and groaned. Someone in the audience shouted, "Send them to Sing Sing," and there was great cheering.

Judge James Emott was called on next. Under his skillful artistry, the crowd grew even more restive and more responsive.

"The world is waiting," Emott said, "to see if the men of New York believe in honesty or worship fraud. We must punish the guilty. We must recover the money back to the city. If there is no law to do it persist . . . agitate, agitate until you get a law. There is no power like the power of people armed, aroused and enkindled with the enthusiasm of a righteous wrath."

Tweed would read those words of course. And one wonders if he remembered other words that were spoken at another meeting. March 5, it was, 1853. James W. Gerard was talking about the Forty Thieves, and his audience, too, was angry: "I behold before me a vast congregation of Kings. All you have to do is will the change . . . will it and you will have it."

That was said of the Forty Thieves. Now it was 1871 and they were talking only of Tweed and his small band of conspirators.

"Hang them!" It was a voice from the audience. And there were cheers. Joseph H. Choate moved to the center of the stage. In his hand was a resolution demanding, among other things, the repeal of the Tweed charter and the recovery of the money that had been stolen. There was a pause. He held the resolution up to the audience.

"This is what we're going to do about it!"

The audience rose to its feet as if in a single gesture and the hall rang with their voices. And the resolution was adopted.

A committee was formed. They called themselves a Committee of Seventy and they were out for blood. Tilden, who had remained in the background until he was certain that Tweed's power was weakened beyond revival, now came to the fore. He wanted to be the one who would get the credit for finally breaking the Tweed Ring. He also wanted to be President of the United States.

Three days after the meeting at Cooper Union, the Committee of Seventy went to court to obtain an injunction restraining the Mayor, and the others in the Ring from spending or collecting any additional city money until further notice. The suit was brought in the name of one John Foley who was chosen for this job because he was a citizen, a taxpayer, and had an Irish name.

Tweed heard about the move and was contemptuous. Didn't they know he owned the courts? Amateurs shouldn't take on professionals. The matter would be argued by former Judge George C. Barrett on the 7th. And the judge before whom he would appear was good old George Barnard, Tweed's friend and appointee. This fight, Tweed was sure, would end like all the others.

He underestimated Tilden who was now working with the Committee of Seventy.

Judge Barrett appeared at the designated time and place. The courtroom was crowded. By the time Judge Barnard entered, every seat was taken and there were scores more standing against the walls. Even the presence of one Jacob Rosenzweig, accused abortionist, in an adjoining courtroom failed to draw the crowds from the drama in Barnard's court.

It was almost like a play. Judge Barnard being asked to grant an injunction that would keep the Ring from their plunder. The spectators listened closely. Judge Barnard would end all this with a few chosen words.

Judge Barrett addressed the court: "We come here fairly and frankly to make our application. The people claim their right and they mean to have it. They ask but justice. We make the application on behalf of a people who have been most mercilessly robbed."

Judge Barnard examined the application. Then the lightning struck.

"You are entitled to this order, Sir," he said. "I will grant the injunction."

There was stunned silence in the courtroom. Then a ripple of applause from those there who were not sympathetic to Tammany or the Ring.

They said that night around the city that Tilden had promised Barnard that he would be nominated for governor.

And that evening Jennings wrote another editorial for the *Times:* "The long night is now vanishing and the dawn of a happier day than we have known for a long period begins to brighten the skies. The Ring may effect to make light of the events now occurring, but their death knell has sounded and well will it be for them if a retribution does not overtake them so fearful as to cause them to be remembered in after times, not only for the magnitude of their crimes but for the solemn warning of their punishment."

Nast published a cartoon showing the Ring members standing in the shadow of the gallows. Hall, Sweeny and Connolly are shown quaking with fear. Not so Tweed. Nast drew him tipping his hat to the noose in splendid impudence. One suspects that, now that the fight was almost over, Nast was sensing a grudging admiration for the very arrogance that had made Tweed the arch-enemy that he was.

A reporter for the *New York Sun* went to Mayor Hall's

office and asked his response to Judge Barnard's action. The Mayor pretended unconcern.

"This Foley," he said, "is a crazy fellow who, I have been told, claims to be a lineal descendant of the youth who fired the Ephesian dome. In its practical effect the granting of the injunction is one of Judge Barnard's stereotype jokes."

Another reporter managed to wedge his way into Tweed's office. He found the Boss looking jovial.

"You don't seem," said the reporter, "to be very downcast."

"I? Pooh! I'm not afraid. What do I care?"

Nobody had said anything about being afraid. Tweed was protesting too strongly.

The reporter pointed out that an article had appeared in a recent edition of the *Nation* hinting that Tweed might be lynched. Tweed answered quickly:

"The man who wrote that knows he told a lie and he wouldn't dare to tell me so to my face. I was born in New York and I mean to stay here, too."

"You don't seem to be afraid of a violent death. Are you?"

Tweed stamped his foot on the floor. "Well, if they want me to come I'll be there . . . I'll be there, Sir."

Suddenly Tweed, the perfect antagonist, was not making much sense. He looked at the reporter for a moment and broke into a smile.

"The *Times*," Tweed went on, "has been saying all along that I have no brains. Well, I'll show Jones that I have brains." Suddenly the smile was gone. "I tell you, Sir, if this man Jones would have said all the things he has said about me twenty-five years ago he wouldn't be alive now. But, you see, when a man has a wife and children, he can't do such a thing."

He was clenching his fists now. "I would have killed him."

But it wasn't twenty-five years earlier. It was September 9, 1871, and time was running out.

On the night of September 10th, someone broke into Comptroller Connolly's office and stole the city vouchers. It was a sloppy move. There were copies at the Broadway Bank. And the real proof was in the ledgers that the *Times* had anyway. The Ring members were beginning to panic.

Mayor Hall, pretending shock over the theft of the vouchers, wrote a letter to Connolly, demanding that he resign. A scapegoat was needed and Connolly was perfect for the role. But Connolly refused. Tilden was advising him now. He was safe. Or so he thought.

Sweeny was the first to go. He went to France. J. H. Ingersoll, who had sold furniture to the city for fabulous prices, also left for France. And Andrew H. Garvey, who had once made $133,187.20 for two days' plastering work for the city, disappeared at about the same time.

Connolly, who was in daily conference now with Tilden, surrendered completely. Tilden had discovered an obscure provision of the law which permitted the comptroller to appoint a deputy to act in his capacity for short periods of time. Connolly talked with Tilden at his home in Gramercy Park and, at his suggestion, turned the functions of his office over to a man named Andrew H. Green. Green was a member of the Committee of Seventy.

The Committee now controlled the city's finances. Mayor Hall refused to recognize the new appointment and sent a prim little note to city departments so indicating. Nobody paid any attention to it. And Green moved in.

Tweed was re-nominated for state senator.

He made his acceptance speech at a rally on the night of September 22nd. The rally was held in Tweed Plaza, and for a moment it looked like the old days. There was a big crowd and plenty of calcium lights. From the platform where

Tweed sat, he could almost see little Cherry Street where he had been born. Nearby was the Bowery, where he had fought so many fires in the old days and so many men, some of whom where in the audience that night cheering him on. Tweed made one of his rare speeches:

"At home again among the friends of my childhood I feel that I can safely place myself, my record and all that I have performed as a public official, plainly and openly to their gaze. Reviled as man has seldom been, traduced as man has seldom been, maligned as man has seldom been, I point proudly to my record to prove my character, and ask only a fair, a bold and a very impartial investigation at an early day of all my official acts and all the records and acts of my life."

Seventy-five hundred dollars for thermometers for the courthouse; $41,746.83 for brooms; carpets that would have covered City Hall Park several times over . . .

Tweed spoke with confidence that night but already he was secretly selling his holdings and transferring the money to his son. He sold his yacht, the big house on Fifth Avenue and Forty-third Street, some stables on Fifty-ninth Street . . .

Tweed was re-elected to the state senate. Everywhere else in the city, Tammany suffered terrible losses. But Tweed was re-elected.

On November 26th, Connolly was sitting in his office talking with Tilden when Sheriff Brennan entered. He touched Connolly on the shoulder and served him with an arrest order. Connolly was dumfounded.

"Mr. Tilden," he said, "I'm arrested!"

Tilden pretended surprise. "No," he said in a shocked voice. "What is the bail, Sheriff?"

"One million dollars!"

Connolly was quite capable of raising six million. But he knew that his enemies would institute attachment proceedings if this were known and so he went reluctantly to jail.

But the Ludlow Street establishment soon proved too onerous for the fun-loving Mr. Connolly and, after Judge Barnard in one last flamboyant gesture, reduced his bail to $500,000, Connolly sadly turned the sum over to Sheriff Brennan and walked out of jail. It was New Year's Eve, 1871. Connolly took one last look at the city, festive now on this holiday eve, and made arrangements to sail immediately for France.

Connolly, Sweeny, Garvey, Ingersoll. The Champs Elysee at apéritif time was beginning to look like Tammany Hall on a Saturday night.

The Committee of Seventy, meanwhile, was working overtime. They enlisted the aid of Charles O'Conor, one of the city's most prominent lawyers. Like Foley, O'Conor was chosen largely because his Irish name would make ineffectual any Tammany charge that resentful Protestantism was behind this whole thing. O'Conor, brilliant and unassailable and charmingly Irish, addressed himself with his usual professional dispatch to the issue at hand, and he was quickly appointed special state attorney general to bring civil suits against Tweed and the others.

He didn't take long. On October 27, 1871, Tweed was arrested and held in one million dollars' bail. The phrase, one million dollars, had a special, almost symbolic, meaning for the nineteenth century. Actually, he did not get anywhere near a cell and the whole thing was done almost like a rehearsal for some ritual whose meaning was obscure and lost in time. Sheriff Brennan, very busy these days, came to Tweed's office with his deputies and bade Tweed a good morning.

"Good morning," Tweed answered. "Take seats, gentlemen."

There was a moment's pause. It was one thirty in the afternoon. A chilly autumn rain was streaking the office windows. Brennan spoke.

"Mr. Tweed, I have an order for your arrest."

"I expected it, but not quite so soon."

Not quite so soon? Actually, the sheriff was late. An order for Tweed's arrest might logically have come nineteen years before.

Jay Gould, who was present, furnished the million dollars immediately, the sheriff departed and the incident was ended —at least for the moment.

The *Times* was exultant and, for once, hardly impartial. "Tweed Under Arrest," was the headline. "Captured in his Den . . . A Day of Heartfelt Rejoicing Among the Better Classes."

On December 15, the Grand Jury returned an indictment against Tweed and three days later handed down two more indictments. The charge was forgery. Then, the same day, there was another indictment charging grand larceny.

Tweed resigned all offices except that of state senator. And suddenly the name Tweed became almost an epithet. Professional politicians could condone thieving easily enough. But they were shocked when the theft was discovered. Tilden men were elected sachems while Tweed became just another crook under indictment. He had taken public money and he had been caught. But it was not his wickedness, in truth, that was his downfall. Rynders had been wicked, and Mayor Wood, and there was no public revulsion against them. Tweed's sin in 1871 was that he had become old-fashioned. Things would not be done his way ever again. He was ultimately understandable in a city of first generation immigrants, of volunteer firemen, of voters who were illiterate and hungry. And his tragedy was that, at forty-eight, he had out-lived his time. He was grotesque and an anachronism and, even as the old city was being torn down and rebuilt, so Tweed had to be destroyed that something else could rise in his place.

On January 7, 1873, Tweed was finally brought to trial. It was in the Court of Oyer and Terminer before Judge Noah Davis. Tilden, who could remember waiting—hat in hand—for an appointment with the Boss in earlier days, was the principal witness against him. And he exulted in the role. Governor? Maybe President? Andrew J. Garvey, whom the *Times* had named the "Prince of Plasterers," came back from Paris and also took the stand. The evidence against Tweed was overwhelming. But the man who had nosed out John Webb for alderman in 1851 was not one to surrender easily. Despite the evidence, despite the judge's instructions to the jury almost demanding a guilty verdict, the jury could not agree. Later it was found that nine stood for acquittal and three for a finding of guilty. Of these three, two said they would vote for acquittal if the third would.

His name has not survived. But whoever he was, he held out. Had he voted with the others, Tweed would have been vindicated and could never again have been brought to trial. But one juror held out and the case could be tried again.

Tweed, however, was exultant. "I am tired of this whole farce," he said. "No jury will ever convict me."

And he took off for California on a pleasure trip.

A second trial was ordered for November 5, 1873. And this time the attorneys for the prosecution were on the alert for any attempt to pack the jury. Young lawyers were hired to watch each prospective juror. And detectives were hired to watch the lawyers. It took nine days to select the panel this time. Even so, one of the jurors had to be dismissed. He was E. H. Lubry, juror number eight. Lubry was seen talking with a police official who later spoke privately with Tweed. The judge censured Lubry and another was selected and the trial began.

It took only four days. Attorneys for the defense spent much of their time preparing to cross-examine Garvey. And they were shocked when the prosecution rested without calling him at all.

The verdict was returned on Wednesday, November 19, 1873. Tweed came into the courtroom at ten. Reporters noticed a dramatic change. His usual cockiness was gone. He appeared nervous and flustered, almost as if he knew that at long, long last the game was over. But for a moment it appeared that his luck might hold. The jury was summoned and advised the judge that they had not been able to reach a decision. They were returned for further deliberation. The rumor circulated around the courtroom that four of the jurors were for acquittal.

At ten forty-five they again filed in and announced that a verdict had been reached.

Guilty.

Tweed was found guilty on one hundred four of one hundred and twenty counts specified in the indictment and was released in the custody of Sheriff Brennan.

Three days later, Tweed was returned to the court for the sentence. Attorneys for the prosecution argued for a cumulative sentence—in this case, inasmuch as some of the counts were related, a sentencing on one hundred and two distinct offenses.

John Graham, attorney for Tweed, sprang to his feet. "Your Honor, we are taught, from the time we enter this world, to ask for mercy; and those prayers which we put in our own behalf must teach us to render deeds of mercy to . . ." He was sobbing and unable to continue. Tweed buried his face in his hands. Some of the spectators were sobbing openly.

Judge Davis was not quite so affected. He peered down at Tweed who stood before him, clutching the back of a chair as if he needed support. A *Times'* reporter watched Tweed's face closely. He wrote that Tweed's face was stolid and his gaze almost vacant. Occasionally his lips quivered.

"William Marcy Tweed," Judge Davis began, "you stand convicted by the verdict of an intelligent and honest jury of the large number of crimes charged against you in the indictment. That verdict, in the opinion of the court, could not have been otherwise without a violation of the oath the jury had taken and an utter disregard of the obligations under which they rested, to speak the truth and the truth only by their verdict."

And there was more. At one point the judge slammed his hand against the bench to emphasize a point and a visible tremor went through Tweed's body.

The sentence was a cumulative one—twelve years in prison and a fine of $12,750. And Tweed was led from the courtroom. There was a scattering of applause at the verdict. That was in his ears as he left for prison.

His pedigree was taken: name, age, address. He was asked his business or profession, and he threw out the answer. "Statesman," he said. Religion? None.

And he was taken to the county penitentiary on Blackwell's Island.

He didn't serve the twelve years. His attorneys appealed the sentence and the Court of Appeals ruled that it should not be in excess of the punishment prescribed for one offense. Tweed paid a $250 fine and on January 15, 1875, was released from prison.

But Tilden had anticipated that. And Tweed was immediately re-arrested on a civil suit to recover $6,000,000 stolen from the city. And this time bail was fixed at $3,000,-000. Tilden, now governor, had done his work well. Three million was a little too much to ask for old time's sake even of Gould, and Tweed, weary now and no longer much of a fighter, was remanded to Ludlow Street Jail to await the slow-turning wheels of justice.

A little too slow for Tweed. Spring came and summer and an autumn sombre with memories of other autumns when the turning of the leaves and the first chilly nights had meant the coming of an election and the excitement of victory.

There were no more victories for Tweed. He was a symbol now. Connolly and Sweeny had fled. Barnard and Cardozo had been impeached. Hall had been tried and found innocent of any misdoings. It would be Tweed who would pay for it all. Governor Tilden wanted it that way. He was, after all, the leader of the Democratic party in New York and if all men who had shared in the untidiness of the Tweed era were to be punished, the shadow would fall very close to the executive mansion. Tilden was governor and Tweed was a prisoner in jail. But they had mutual friends . . .

It was an odd sort of jail. Tweed's cell was the former quarters of the warden and his family. And Tweed was accustomed to taking an outing at regular intervals. In the company of a sheriff and deputy, he would frequently have a ride through the city, a stroll in Central Park maybe, and dinner at home before returning to his cell for the night. It was an arrangement that, for a man of Tweed's imagination, had all sorts of potential.

On December 4, 1875, Tweed, his son, William, Jr., the warden and a keeper went for a drive. They toured the upper sections of the city and then, as dusk fell, returned to the home of Tweed's son on Madison Avenue near Sixtieth Street. They entered and cigars were passed and Tweed, after a moment, excused himself and went upstairs to talk with his wife.

It was a brownstone house that differed little from its neighbors. It was four stories high with the usual stoop and basement. There were two parlors on the first floor, with a bay window in the back. Upstairs there were bedrooms and another sitting room. And—there was a back door.

At about six-twenty, five minutes after Tweed had gone upstairs, the warden asked young Tweed to summon his father. It was time to return to Ludlow Street. Young Tweed went upstairs and after a pause returned to the parlor. His father, he announced, was not there.

Actually, at that moment he was still quite close. The escape had been neatly arranged and there were no hitches. Tweed had simply hurried out the back door to the street where a carriage was waiting. At a signal, he jumped in and, by that gesture, he became a fugitive for whom there would be no rest until he died.

His movements are confused; he never revealed the precise details. Indications are that he was rowed across the Hudson to a hiding place in the flats of New Jersey. From there, he went into hiding on Staten Island where a small coastal craft took him to Florida.

The authorities offered a ten thousand dollar reward for his recapture. But it was a feeble gesture. So many people would be made happy by his death. So many memories could be laid to rest. So many stories would never be told. So many names never mentioned.

He didn't die. Not yet. From Florida he went to Cuba where, after a brief arrest because authorities discovered he had no Spanish visa, he was pardoned and allowed to sail for Spain. It was a good choice. There was no extradition treaty with Spain at the time and the Spanish were usually sympathetic to "political refugees." And New York and the Bowery and the Seventh Ward and the squat, ugly little county courthouse were far away.

On June 27, 1876, Tilden was nominated for the Presidency by the Democratic Party. Tweed had hoped to pick the President that year. But he was not present at the convention. He was in an odorous little jail in Santiago. He said later that he made dominoes out of cloth and so beguiled the time.

Nast was not pleased with the nomination nor with Tilden's role. He published a cartoon showing Tweed in convict's striped uniform picking up two little urchins from the street. And he was saying to them: "If all the people want is to have somebody arrested, I'll have you plunderers convicted. You will be allowed to escape; nobody will be hurt; and then Tilden will go to the White House and I to Albany as Governor." There is a sign on the wall behind him: "It takes a thief or one who has been associated with thieves to catch a thief." And the whole thing is captioned: "Tweed-le-dee and Tilden-dum."

The cartoon did not help Tilden's campaign. Although he won a popular majority, he lost in the electoral college and Rutherford B. Hayes became President.

And the cartoon had a disastrous effect on the career of William Marcy Tweed. Spanish authorities had been advised that it was believed that Tweed was en route to their shores, and it was requested that, on arrival, he be arrested and turned over to the American authorities. No photograph of Tweed was available in Spain but copies of the "Tweed-le-dee and Tilden-dum" cartoon were distributed. The Spanish customs men, unable to read English, interpreted the posture of Tweed with the two little urchins as that of a kidnapper and, while Spaniards had a certain sympathy for political refugees, they had none for one who would visit violence on children. When Tweed arrived at Vigo, Spain, he was promptly arrested and lodged in the old fortress there. And he probably never knew why his jailers treated him with such contempt.

The U.S.S. *Franklin* was dispatched to Spain to bring Tweed back to New York. His arrival was strangely symbolic.

As Tweed descended the gangplank, it began to shake under his weight. This caused Tweed to lose his balance and he had to run down to keep on his feet. And so he came back to New York, running down the gangplank and across the dock where he fell headlong into a pile of coal. He arose slowly and the authorities came forward and, as he was again arrested, he was trying vainly to wipe the dirt from his clothes.

The city that he came back to was in some ways as strange as the city he had left. Cherry Street, the Bowery, the whole Seventh Ward had been lost, almost, and had only remembered importance in this new city uptown. A young man named Thomas Edison was experimenting with an incandescent lamp and would soon start a company to provide certain sections of the city with a light that used no fuel and could not be blown out. An elevated railroad ran along Greenwich Street from the Battery to Fifty-ninth Street. And the city was getting as sophisticated as Paris and London. Already the streetcars ran all night on Third and Eighth Avenues.

The New York Life Insurance Company announced cash assets that year of $31,000,000.

The street system extended to Harlem and the population had finally exceeded a million. And there were twenty-six newspapers published every day.

Irish and German immigration had fallen off dramatically, but there was a new influx. Italians this time. And an Irish name on the Tammany ticket was no longer an absolute guarantee of success. It was a city where the rich had large homes characterized by Moorish fret works, "cozy corners" and innumerable rubber plants. The middle class were experimenting with the newly introduced folding wall bed and the poor had dreams, not of taking over the city but of themselves becoming rich.

Kids no longer roasted potatoes and pigs' tails on the high ground north of Fourteenth Street. It was a city park now.

And New York Society had picked up its skirts and moved uptown. Even the business areas were on streets that Tweed could remember as being farmland. And there was a new name in New York in 1876—the "Tenderloin." That was the area roughly from Twenty-fourth to Fortieth Streets between Fifth and Seventh Avenues. It was so named because of its potential in official graft. A police captain, A. S. Williams, who had been transferred to the West Thirtieth Street Station after a long career in the outskirts, is alleged to have remarked: "I've been on chuck steak ever since I've been on the force and now I'm going to get a bit of the Tenderloin."

Cherry Street was there, and the Bowery, and they probably looked much as they looked in past times. But it was 1876, and the city had grown and left them behind.

Tweed went back to jail. He volunteered to confess everything and was a little disappointed, one suspects, to find out that no one cared any more to hear his story.

Connolly stayed in Paris and enjoyed his fortune. Sweeny gave back $394,594.28 of the money he had stolen and blamed it all on his dead brother. He was allowed to return. Another of the Ring collectors paid $150,387.90 and was forgiven and welcomed back to the fold. The executors of the estate of Watson, the late county auditor, paid out $558,237, and there were several other payments. Former Mayor Hall was not sued at all. He stayed in New York, pranced up and down Fifth Avenue and, when things got boring, wrote a play.

The sums returned to the city, less counsel fees, amounted to $1,121,720.75. The amount stolen was somewhere between $45,000,000 and $75,000,000.

Tweed, back at the Ludlow Street Jail, realized that he had a bad heart condition. And a diabetic condition, which had first showed itself on Blackwell's Island, began to be acute. Tweed testified before a committee of the Board of Aldermen investigating the Ring, but his testimony was unspectacular and he gave it only on the expectation that he would be released.

He wasn't. In the winter of 1877—1878, Tweed had several bad heart attacks. On April 3, 1878, he celebrated his fifty-fifth birthday with a little party in jail. That was on a Wednesday. On the following Friday, a doctor examined him and found that his heart was in a serious condition. There was also a mild case of bronchial pneumonia. But as yet, it was not serious.

But the pain in his heart persisted and got worse. Some of his friends told authorities that Tweed would never get well in the dank condition of the jail. But nothing was done. Tweed belonged to the past. And he was something that his generation did not wish to be reminded of. The newly invented telephone was becoming a practical necessity and the first commercial telephone exchange had been opened that year in New Haven. New Yorkers were not talking much about Tweed. They were talking about a recent invention of George Eastman. It was a photographic plate that was dry. Soon anyone could take pictures. And a new musical play, *H.M.S. Pinafore,* was going to open soon in New York after a successful run in London. Harrigan and Hart, a New York vaudeville team, introduced a new dance in their act that year. It was called "Walkin' da Cake," and soon the cake walk and its emphasis on syncopation was all the rage. The signs on some Sixth Avenue cars, "This Car for Colored Persons Only," were beginning to seem odd to New Yorkers and in that year a man named Henry O. Flipper became the first Negro to graduate from West Point. On January 10th, a senator named A. A. Sargeant introduced a bill into Congress that would give women the right to vote.

There was one item in the papers that could evoke memories. There were epidemics of yellow fever in Memphis, Tennessee, and in New Orleans. Surely his mother and father must have told Tweed about the summer before he was born, and how the fever crept slowly north and east until it came down their street and knocked at their neighbor's door. It started on Rector Street. There was a family named Reder and one day one of the daughters complained of being ill . . .

On April 11, 1878, Tweed began to die. He had a bad night, but when dawn came he was still stubbornly alive. A doctor dispatched a servant for a fly blister. It seemed to help. But at eight thirty, Tweed told the doctor that he was going to die.

One of his daughters came to visit him that morning and, in the half light, failed to see the change that had come over her father. She stayed for a moment and then went out to get him some ice cream.

It was a few seconds to noon when she returned. The doctor was there and some others. Tweed was lying on his left side with his face cradled in his hand. And he was really dying at last. His daughter saw his face and dropped her package. The ice cream and some little cakes spilled across the floor.

Suddenly the room was filled with sound. It was the clock at the tower of the nearby Essex Market. The waves of sound rolled through the room. And when they were done, Tweed was dead.

It was a modest funeral. The Reverend Dr. Price, who had officiated at Tweed's marriage and the marriage of his daughter and had baptized each of the eight children, read the Office of the Dead. Burial was in Greenwood Cemetery in Brooklyn. The funeral was private and dignified. There was only one incident to mar the solemnity of the occasion. The family had requested that when the funeral procession passed City Hall, the flag there might be lowered to half mast.

The request was denied.

BIBLIOGRAPHY

Asbury, Herbert, *The Gangs of New York, An Informal History of the Under-world*. New York and London: Alfred A. Knopf, 1927.

Baker, General L. C., *History of the United States Secret Service*. Philadelphia: L. C. Baker, 1867.

Berger, Meyer, *The Story of the New York Times 1851-1951*. Simon and Schuster, New York, 1951.

Behil, Book of, *A Narrative in Biblical Form of Part of the Career of Wm. M. Tweed*. New York: 1875.

Blake, E. Vale, *History of the Tammany Society from its Organization to the Present Time, 1901*. New York: 1901.

Booth, Mary L., *History of the City of New York*. New York: James Miller, 1863.

Bowen, Croswell, *The Elegant Oakey*. New York: Oxford University Press, 1956.

Brace, Charles Loring, *The Dangerous Classes of New York*. Wynkoop & Hollenbeck, 1872.

Breen, Matthew P., *Thirty Years of New York Politics Up To Date*. New York: The Author, 1899.

Brown, T. Alliston, *A History of the New York Stage from the First Performance in 1732 to 1901*. 1903.

Bryce, James, *The American Commonwealth*. London: Macmillan and Company, 1888.

Costello, Augustine E., *Our Police Protectors. History of the New York Police from the Earliest Period to the Present Time*. Published by the author, 1885.

Davenport, John I., *The Election and Naturalization Frauds in New York City, 1860-1870*. New York: 1894.

Davis, Elmer, *A History of the New York Times*. New York: The New York Times, 1921.

Dunshee, Kenneth Holcomb, *As You Pass By*. New York: Hastings House, 1952.

Flick, Alexander C., *History of the State of New York. Volume VII.* New York: 1933-1937.

Genung, Abram Polhemus, *The Frauds of the New York City Government Exposed. Sketches of the Members of the Ring and Their Confederates.* New York: The Author, 1871.

Hall, A. Oakey, Scrapbooks of clippings relating to the career of A. Oakey Hall. New York: 1857-1874. New York Public Library.

Harlow, Alvin F., *Old Bowery Days. The Chronicles of a Famous Street.* New York & London: D. Appleton and Company, 1931.

Harper's Weekly, Vol. XXI, p. 284, 1877, *William M. Tweed, Romance of His Flight and Exile.*

Haswell, Charles H., *Reminiscences of an Octogenarian.* New York: Harper and Brothers, 1897.

Hatcher, William B., *Edward Livingston, Jeffersonian Republican and Jacksonian Democrat.* Louisiana State University Press, 1940.

Hawley, Walter L., *What New York Owes to Tweed.* Munsey Magazine, Vol. XXXVI, pp. 616-620. New York: 1907.

Headley, J. T., *The Great Riots of New York, 1712 to 1873.* New York, E. B. Treat, 1873.

Hirsch, Mark D., *More Light on "Boss" Tweed.* Political Science Quarterly.

Home, Rufus, *The Story of Tammany,* Harper's Magazine, 1872.

Hone, Philip, Diary of, 1828-1851. New York: Dodd, Mead and Company, 1889.

Hunt, Charleston Havens, *Life of Edward Livingston.* New York: D. Appleton & Co., 1864.

Josephson, Matthew, *The Robber Barons. The Great American Capitalists, 1861-1901.* New York: Harcourt, Brace and Company, 1934.

Kouwenhoven, John A., *The Columbia Historical Portrait of New York.* Garden City, New York: Doubleday & Company, 1953.

Lewis, Alfred Henry, *The Boss and How He Came to Rule New York.* New York: A. L. Burt Co., 1903.

Linton, William James, *The House that Tweed Built.* Cambridge, Mass.: published by the author, 1871.

Lynch, Denis Tilden, *"Boss" Tweed.* New York: Boni and Liveright, 1927.

Martin, Edward Winslow, *The Secrets of the Great City: A Work Descriptive of the Virtues and the Vices, the Mysteries, Miseries and Crimes of New York City.* Philadelphia, Pa.; Cincinnati, Ohio; Chicago, Ill.; St. Louis, Mo.; Atlanta, Ga., Jones, Brothers & Co., 1868.

Moody, Richard, *The Astor Place Riot.* Bloomington: Indiana University Press, 1958.

Myers, Gustavus, *The History of Tammany Hall.* New York: Boni and Liveright, Incorporated, 1917.

The National Cyclopedia of American Biography.

New York (County) Courts: Court of General Sessions. . . . *Wonderful trial of Caroline Lohman, alias Restell with speeches of counsel, charge of Court and verdict of jury (reported in full for the National Police Gazette)* . . . New York City: Burgess, Stringer and Co., 1847.

New York in Slices: By an Experienced Carver: Being the Original Slices Published in the New York Tribune. (George G. Foster, Author?) New York: Garrett & Co., 22 Ann Street, 1852.

The Old Brewery, and the New Mission House at the Five Points, By Ladies of the Mission. New York: Stringer & Townsend, 1854.

Orth, Samuel P., *The Boss and the Machine, A Chronicle of the Politicians and Party Organization.* Yale University Press, 1919.

Paine, Albert Bigelow, *Th. Nast, His Period and His Pictures.* New York: The Macmillan Company, 1904.

Parton, James, *How New York City Is Governed.* Boston: Ticknor and Fields, 1866.

Polhemus, J., *Peculation Triumphant; Being the Record of a Four Years' Campaign Against Official Malversation in the City of New York. A.D. 1871 to 1875.* New York: J. Polhemus, Printer, 1875.

Report of the Special Committee of the Board of Aldermen Appointed to Investigate the "Ring" Frauds, Together with the Testimony Elicited During the Investigation. Board of Aldermen, January 4, 1878, Document No. 8, New York, 1878.

Riordan, William L., *Plunkett of Tammany Hall, A Series of Very Plain Talks on Very Practical Politics, Delivered by Ex-Senator George Washington Plunkett, the Tammany Philosopher, from His Rostrum—the New York County Court-house Bootblack Stand—and Recorded by William L. Riordan,* New York: 1905. McClure, Phillips and Company.

Robinson, Solon, *Hot Corn: Life Scenes in New York Illustrated.* New York: De Witt and Davenport, 1854.

Ross, Joel H., M.D., *What I Saw in New York; or a Bird's Eye View of City Life.* Auburn, N. Y.: Derby & Miller, 1851.

Smith, Matthew Hale, *Sunshine and Shadow in New York.* Hartford: J. B. Burr and Company, 1869.

Steffens, Lincoln, *The Shame of the Cities.* New York: 1904. (New York: Peter Smith, 1948.)

Steffens, Lincoln, *The Struggle for Self-Government.* New York: McClure, Phillips and Company, 1906.

The Strangers' Hand-Book for the City of New York; or, What to See and How to See it. C. S. Francis & Co., 1845.

Swanberg, W. A., *Jim Fisk: The Career of an Improbable Rascal,* New York: Charles Scribner's Sons, 1959.

Tilden, Samuel J., *The New York City Ring, Its Origin, Maturity and Fall.* New York: J. Polhemus, 1873.

Townsend, Hon. John D., *New York in Bondage.* New York: 1901.

Van Wyck, Frederick, *Recollections of an Old New Yorker.* New York: Liveright, Inc., 1932.

Wallace, Irving, *The Fabulous Showman. The Life and Times of P. T. Barnum.* New York: Alfred A. Knopf, 1959.

Walling, George W., *Recollections of a New York Chief of Police.* New York: Caxton Book Concern, Limited, 1887.

Werner, M. R., *Tammany Hall.* Garden City, New York: Doubleday, Doran & Company, Inc., 1928.

Werstein, Irving, *July, 1863. The Incredible Story of the Bloody New York City Draft Riots.* New York: Julian Messner, Inc., 1957.

White, Bouck, *The Book of Daniel Drew, A Glimpse of the Fisk-Gould-Tweed Regime From the Inside.* New York: Doubleday, Page and Co., 1910.

Wingate, Charles F., *An Episode in Municipal Government. The Tweed Ring. North American Review,* Vol. CXIX, p. 359; Vol. CXX, p. 119; Vol. CXXI, p. 113.

Wood, Fernando, *A Biography of Fernando Wood, A History of the Forgeries, Perjuries, and Other Crimes of Our "Model" Mayor.* A Pamphlet by Abijah Ingraham, not signed.

Wood, Fernando, *Annual Message of His Honor the Mayor, Fernando Wood, January 7, 1861. Documents of the Board of Aldermen, Part I, January to July 1861, Vol. XXVIII, Document No. 1.*

Wood, Fernando, *Oration Delivered by Hon. Fernando Wood, on the Anniversary of Washington's Birthday, February 22, 1862, at Scranton, Pa.* New York: 1862.

Much of the material for this book was derived from contemporary accounts of the incidents involved. The following newspapers were consulted: New York *Spectator, Morning Courier* and New York *Enquirer,* New York *Daily Advertiser,* New York *Herald,* New York *Post, Sun, New York Times,* New York *Tribune.*

The author expresses his thanks to Columbia University for granting him access to the splendid Kilroe Tammany Collection, Butler Library.